Madeleine

*A most heartbreaking
and extraordinary
disappearance*

**EXPRESS
NEWSPAPERS**

This book first published in 2007 by
Express Newspapers
The Northern & Shell Building
10 Lower Thames Street
London EC3R 6EN

ISBN-13: 978-0-85079-348-2

Internal design and typesetting by Andrew Barker
Cover design by Richard Green

Printed and bound in Poland. Produced by Polskabook.

Contents

Maddy's gone!

The sun had set over the little Portuguese resort of Praia da Luz. The date was 3 May 2007, and Kate and Gerry McCann, two British doctors on holiday with their three children and friends, were dining in the tapas bar of the Ocean Club resort in which they were staying on the Algarve. The couple's three children were tucked up safely nearby: every half an hour, Kate or Gerry would slip away from the table to make sure all was well.

But at about 10.00pm on that fateful night, it suddenly became apparent that all was not well – far from it. Kate, who had gone to check up on the children, suddenly appeared, distraught. Her oldest daughter, Madeleine, had disappeared from the bedroom she was sharing with her two siblings, and Kate was, unsurprisingly, beside herself. But what happened next has been the subject of an enormous amount of debate. Kate was shrieking something that, according to later reports, was either, 'Maddy's gone!' or 'They've taken her!'. Whichever it was, Kate was clearly acting under extreme stress, but in later months, as the mystery deepened, some people began to believe that those words had a particular significance. The whole incident was to blow up into global news: a little girl vanished without trace in the middle of a crowded holiday resort, while her parents were dining nearby. What possibly could have happened?

Right from the start, the case seemed extraordinary. The Ocean Club had been purpose built in the 1980s to appeal to families exactly like the McCanns. Based around a little fishing village on the Algarve, the complex was spread across Praia da Luz, and the family was staying in an apartment in the central area of the village. Most of the other apartments in the village were privately owned. During the summer months, tourists dominated the village, the majority being British. There was even a British pub, The Bull, for holidaymakers to use.

And it was an attractive resort. The buildings, which were set up around landscaped gardens including three swimming pools and five tennis courts, were built to look like traditional Portuguese and Moorish buildings. Most had views of the nearby Luz beach and Atlantic Ocean. There were poolside snack bars and activities on offer including sailing and windsurfing. It was the last type of place you would expect a tragedy such as this to occur.

And the McCann family seemed odd candidates to be

caught up in such a drama. Gerry and Kate McCann, both 38, from Rothley village near Leicester, were doctors: he a heart specialist at Leicester's Glenfield Hospital and his wife a GP in Melton Mowbray. The family could not have been more normal: Madeleine was just a week shy of her fourth birthday, and had been sleeping in her white pyjamas next to Amelie and Sean, her two-year-old twin brother and sister. It was all quite bizarre.

Indeed, the McCanns themselves didn't seem to know what to make of it. They were caught in the eye of a storm, trying to cope with this unexpected and terrible development, and found themselves in a global spotlight that otherwise never would have been theirs. But cope they did, managing to talk publicly about their plight from early on. Gerry was the first to do so.

'First of all, we would like to thank everyone here in Portugal, the UK and elsewhere for all your support during this extremely difficult time for our family,' said Dr McCann. 'We are pleased that the family liaison officers from Leicestershire are now working closely with the Portuguese police in keeping us informed. We have no further information regarding the investigation but appreciate the significant effort everyone is making on our behalf. We would again like to appeal for any information, however small, that may lead to the safe return of

Madeleine. Finally we would like to thank the media for respecting our privacy, especially that of Madeleine's little brother and sister.'

Further details began to emerge. The Mark Warner resort actually offered childcare in the evenings, a room-listening service, in which nannies moved from room to room checking on children from 8.00pm to midnight, or a crèche where parents could leave their children from 7.30pm to 11.30pm, and in which they could either be entertained with films and video or allowed to sleep. In addition to that, paid-for babysitters were available and there was widespread confusion as to why the McCanns had used none of that.

Other members of the family began to explain what had happened. 'The phone went last night and it was my brother Gerry, distraught on the phone, breaking his heart,' said Trish Cameron, Maddy's aunt, who lives in Dunbarton near Glasgow. 'He said, "Madeleine's been abducted, she's been abducted." They kept going back to check the kids every half hour.' When Kate had gone into the room at 10.00pm, however, Madeleine had not been there. 'The door was lying open, the window in the bedroom and the shutters had been jimmied open,' Trish continued. 'Nothing had been touched in the apartment, no valuables taken, no passports. They think someone must have come in the window or gone out the door with her. It looks as if someone's been watching, or they've targeted her.'

A member of the Portuguese police, who were initially very supportive towards the McCanns, confirmed what had happened. 'They immediately raised the alarm and a search was begun, but so far there has been absolutely no sign of the girl,' he said. 'The fear is, she has been abducted.'

Certainly a full-scale police hunt had begun. Specialist anti-kidnap officers from Britain's Serious Organised Crime Agency were already on their way to the Portuguese resort. On the night in question, fellow guests had joined in a search of the grounds that went on until 4.30am. The five-storey block in which the family was staying had been sealed off: forensic specialists were examining the window-sill and three police cars, with a further three police vans, were in attendance. There were concerns that Maddy might have wandered off: the complex was close to the sea, but almost everyone involved – the authorities and, above all, the McCanns – were convinced Maddy had been kidnapped.

The resort itself did all it could to help. 'It was a very emotional and very frantic night and everyone did a fantastic job of getting involved and trying to search the area,' said John Hill, manager of the resort, as events unfolded. 'As you can imagine, Madeleine's parents are distraught and not doing very well at all.' By this time, Maddy's grandparents,

Brian and Susan Healy, from Mossley Hill, Liverpool, were also on their way out to the resort.

In what was to become a pattern in the months ahead, friends of the McCanns spoke out when Gerry and Kate were too shell shocked to do so themselves. 'They were watching the hotel room and going back every half-hour,' said Jill Renwick, a good friend of the couple. 'They went out about eight, went back at nine, they were fine, went back in at ten and she was gone. They are very, very anxious parents and very careful and they chose Mark Warner because it is a family-friendly resort.'

Another friend, Pat Perkins, stepped up to their defense. 'Gerry and Kate are fantastic parents and could see the bedroom from the hotel restaurant,' she said. 'Madeleine's a beautiful little girl. It's her fourth birthday soon. They were supposed to be flying home tomorrow to celebrate. We can't believe what's happening. We've sat by the phone waiting to hear news. We're all going through hell.'

Another holidaymaker, who was in residence at the time, also gave an account of what had happened. 'The parents left the door ajar so they could keep going over and looking at her,' said Mark McCarrick. 'We are hoping that because the door was open, she just walked out.'

In the days that followed, the world itself seemed to go into shock. To disappear without trace, from the middle of a packed holiday complex, seemed utterly inexplicable and indeed, it brought back memories of a similar tragedy that had happened many years earlier when the toddler Ben Needham, who was twenty-one months old at the time, went missing while his family were on holiday in 1991 on the Grecian island of Kos.

'My heart goes out to these poor parents,' said Ben's mother Kerry, who now lives in Sheffield, as the news of Maddy's disappearance spread. 'I know what hell they will be going through. The memories come flooding back all those years to when Ben disappeared. It will be a nightmare for them. They will be distraught, they will blame them-selves, they will feel absolutely helpless and they will be praying that their little girl is found safe and well. All they can do is rely on the police and other support services. She has gone missing in a busy commercial area with good com-munications, so she can be found quickly. Hopefully, they are getting better support from the police than we did. We were in a very remote spot on Kos. I always hoped that Ben would be found quickly, but he disappeared without trace. I still think of him most days and imagine what he looks like now; he will be nearly nineteen. It never goes away and I firmly believe I will see him again one day. But life has to go on and you have to pick up the pieces, although it has taken me a long time to feel like that.'

It would have been little consolation to the McCanns. As the hours following Maddy's disappearance lengthened into days, it emerged that the police believed she might have been kidnapped by a paedophile and that she may well still be held close to the hotel. Further rumours emerged that there was, in fact, a suspect already, although no names were to be issued yet to the press. However, a chaotic press conference was held on the steps of a police station in Portimao, two days after Maddy vanished, in which the police put forth their case.

'There is a prime suspect,' said Guilhermino Encarnacao, director of the judicial police in the Faro region of Portugal. 'There is a portrait sketch of the subject, but I am not going to release it because it may put the little girl's life in danger. Yes, I believe she is still alive. However, in Portugal, such kidnappings are not only for money, they can be for sexual abuse. I cannot deny we are looking for a paedophile.'

Even as early as this, however, criticism began to emerge that the police had not acted fast, or thoroughly, enough. Within the McCann circle there were mutterings that the search was upgraded to a major one only after the intervention of Britain's ambassador to Portugal, John Buck (a fact which, incidentally, makes it look even less likely that Madeleine's parents had anything to do with her disappearance. The family was desperate for help).

Certainly, the mood in Praia da Luz was becoming quite feverish. It was said that more than thirty witnesses had given the police a description of this mysterious suspect – indeed, reading some reports at the time, the impression was that the police had all but got their man. And kind strangers continued to give all the help they could. 'I came here first on Friday morning,' said Dave Shelton, originally from Manchester, who lived in the village. 'I speak a little Portuguese and was helping police knock on all the doors of the apartments. Then people just started coming out of the woodwork, saying, "We've heard, what can we do to help?"'

By this stage sniffer dogs had been brought in (something else to bear in mind by conspiracy theorists who later alleged the McCanns had hidden Madeleine's body in their apartment – the dogs certainly didn't notice), while the family itself, all plans to return to England completely destroyed, moved into another flat not far from where they had been staying. There were quite heartbreaking scenes of Kate and Gerry moving buckets and spades to the place they were to call home for the next four months – and still no progress was made.

Indeed, even at this early stage, there were doubts that the Portuguese police had handled the situation particularly well. While the McCanns themselves were careful not to voice any criticism, their family members felt no such constraints. 'My brother is at his wits' end,' said Gerry's sister Philomena, speaking from Glasgow. 'They've just played it down from the minute he first approached them. I mean, you can hear his voice breaking. His wife, she can barely stand up. She can't sleep; she can't eat. They spent seven hours in the police station yesterday. What for? It took three hours just to get a statement from Kate, and Kate is an extremely articulate young woman. What's going on?'

What indeed? And while the McCanns were being supported by wellwishers across the globe, they were having to contend with something else with now – criticism for leaving the children alone. There were, after all, various types of crèche and babysitting services available, and mutterings were beginning to surface about why the couple hadn't made use of these. The family, understandably, was furious. 'Kate and Gerry are highly responsible parents, very much devoted to the family idea,' said Maddy's uncle, Bryan Kennedy. 'We understand that it is a pleasant resort that is supposed to be safe for families – just the type of place where you can put your children to bed and keep popping back to make sure they were safe.'

Criticism, however, was not the sole preserve of the McCanns. By the time the search had reached its fourth day, the Portuguese police were coming under further attack. It emerged that they had taken twenty-four hours to alert the border police to the news of Maddy's disappearance, raising the fear that she had been smuggled into another country, a fear that was going to intensify over the coming months. The police themselves, meanwhile, were maintaining that Madeleine could still be in the nearby vicinity, perhaps as close as three miles away. The strain on the McCanns was beginning to tell: four days after Maddy had gone missing, the couple – devout Catholics – attended a church service in the Church of Our Lady of Light, in which prayers were said for the missing child.

It was an emotional service for many reasons. It was Dia de Mae in Portugal – Mother's Day – and traditionally children would give their mothers a posy of flowers during the service as a sign of love and to say, 'thank you'. The priest, Father Jose Pacheco, had warned Kate about this in advance, and in the event, a fourteen-year old altar girl, Emily Seromenho, who had an English mother and a Portuguese father, took Madeleine's place to give Kate a posy. 'It is Mother's Day in Portugal,' said Emily. 'It is traditional at Mass that we bring flowers and give them to our mothers and they lay them at the feet of a statue of the Virgin Mary. It is a way of saying, "Thank you for being my mother." It is a special day. It is nice – but today it was sad too, because of what is happening to Madeleine.'

Father Jose also spoke of the missing child. 'We were with the family from the moment of the event,' he told the 150-strong congregation in a service that lasted for ninety minutes. 'You can't be indifferent. Our heart is full of compassion.'

Kate emerged from the church, clutching her daughter's favourite toy, a pink cuddly kitten, and spoke for the first time about what the family was going through. 'Gerry and I would just like to express our sincere gratitude, and thanks to everybody, particularly the local community here who have offered us so much support,' she said. 'We could not have asked for more. Thank you. Please continue to pray for Madeleine. She is lovely.' Her husband also spoke. 'From today's service the things we are going to take are strength, courage and hope,' he said. 'We continue to hope for the best possible outcome from this, for us and for Madeleine.'

They were supported by eight members of their family and friends; meanwhile it was announced that a £100,000 reward had been offered for Maddy's return. A new photograph of the child was released: it showed Maddy in a sun hat, clutching three tennis balls. There were rumours that someone had seen a man leave the complex a few days earlier clutching a little girl by the hand. The mystery deepened further still.

Back in Britain, friends and family of the McCanns

marked Maddy's disappearance. About three hundred people met at the entrance to Leicester's Glenfield Hospital –
where Gerry is a consultant cardiologist – and said prayers.
A candlelit vigil was held in the family's home village of
Rothley, in which residents lit candles and tied yellow ribbons around the village's war memorial, which was a short
distance from where the family lived.

By now, three family liaison officers from the
Leicestershire police had arrived to help the McCanns,
along with two specially-trained counselors who had flown
over from Britain. The McCanns needed all the support
they could get: Kate now made an emotional plea on television, asking for her daughter's safe return. 'Madeleine
is a beautiful, bright, funny and caring little girl,' she said.
'She is so special. Please, please do not hurt her. Please don't
scare her. Please tell us where to find her or put her in a
place of safety and let somebody know where she is. We beg
you to let Madeleine come home. Sean and Amelie need
Madeleine and Madeleine needs us. Please give our little
girl back.' Later claims that the McCanns themselves had
anything to do with their daughter's disappearance look
even more hollow in the light of that: Kate was a doctor, not
an actress. It is almost impossible to believe she was putting
that on.

Further details emerged. The family issued a description

of what exactly Madeleine had been wearing on the night she vanished: white pyjama bottoms with a small floral design and a short-sleeved pink top with a picture of Eyore from Winnie the Pooh. Eyore was also written on the top. These details, evidence of an utterly normal middle-class family on holiday, gained an added piquancy set against Maddy's disappearance: how could something so strange have happened to such a normal family?

And now, for the first time, the possibility arose that it might be too late. On the one hand, the Portuguese police continued to talk about a specific, as yet unnamed, suspect; on the other, Marques Pereira, harbour captain at the nearby Lagos marina, admitted they were now searching for a body. The scene seemed to grow ever more bizarre.

Certainly, all manner of rumours were beginning to emerge. There were reports that Maddy had been taken by an international paedophile ring, which was operating in Portugal because of its lax sex offence laws. There were said to be strong British connections, and Scotland Yard had given the Portuguese police information about sex offenders who regularly went to the Algarve. The international police continued to get involved: the latest to fly out from Britain to help the local police were two child exploitation experts, experienced in profiling offenders.

The local police themselves were subject to increasingly harsh words. A chaotic press conference was staged in which Chief Inspector Olegario Sousa announced, 'The only clues we have found so far are in the apartment' before refusing to disclose what those clues were. He then marched out of the press conference after being angered by journalists' questions.

The local laws were also causing problems. In Portugal, under the law of 'Judicial Secrecy', it is illegal to release details of a police investigation. Bizarrely, that meant that the police could not make public suspicious sightings or issue information about a suspect's description. The police had an artist's impression of the suspect, but they were unable to release it under the law. Nor had missing posters been put up. Many felt the police were being far too casual about the investigation to date.

What was also now becoming clear was that this story had a resonance very few other stories have had. Children, sadly, go missing all the time, but this incident was so strange, so inexplicable – the sheer size and variety of the rumours that were to grow in later months was proof of that – and so downright bizarre it was gripping the world's imagination in a way few other stories would. One sign of this was the number of well known names who were willing to become involved with the case, one of the first being the Portuguese football player Cristiano Ronaldo. At the request of Kate and Gerry, the Manchester United star issued an appeal broadcast in both Portuguese and English: 'I was very upset to hear of the abduction of Madeleine McCann and I appeal to anyone with information to come forward. Please come forward.'

As the search widened, the focus shifted to employees at the Ocean Club resort. It was reported that thirty-one British members of staff had been questioned, along with 120 local employees, who had been asked to show their identification. Stories continued to circulate to the effect that a man had been seen acting suspiciously at the resort, but that the police had failed to do anything about it.

One section of the community that did not appear to be so touched by Madeleine's disappearance, however, was the Portuguese press. Perhaps it was a reaction to some sort of national embarrassment that such a crime had been committed on their shores, or that the local police seemed so incompetent, but the Portuguese press turned on the McCanns very early, accusing them, if not of actually being involved in their daughter's disappearance, then at least of being bad parents. It was routine, they said, for the couple to leave their children alone while they dined with friends. 'Police have reconstructed the holiday routines of the McCanns and have come to the conclusion that the children were left alone on other occasions,' the newspaper *Correio da Manha* wrote, adding that the couple often dined with friends by the pool while their children slept alone. Nor had they expressed concerns to members of staff about leaving their children at night. It was an ugly twist of events, and not one that found favour back home.

Kate's mother Susan Healy, 61, from Woolton in Liverpool, was the first to react strongly to any suggestion that it was the parents who were to blame. 'Their children are IVF children, they waited a long time for them and they are so precious,' she said. 'Why would you think something like this would happen? You make a decision and think it's okay. This time it wasn't and Kate and Gerry have to live with that. That's dreadful and they don't need pressure from people saying they made a mistake. They know this was a mistake. But it wasn't child neglect, it wasn't not caring for your children. Their children are the most important things in their lives. I haven't thought about her birthday on Saturday. I'm just hoping and praying we're going to have her back before then.'

Other family members also sprang to their defence, insisting that the couple had been cheered by the international reaction to their plight and were still hopeful Maddy would be found. 'My brother's a fantastic guy and Kate's a wonderful woman,' said Maddy's uncle John McCann. 'They're great for coming up with positive ideas and they're mobilising contacts all over the place to get as much information and as many leads fed back.'

Maddy's aunt, Philomena McCann, was similarly positive. 'We need to get Madeleine back,' she said, revealing plans to circulate a global e-mail to help publicise the plight of the missing child. 'We must find her. It's not an option to lose her. The whole family needs her here. We all love children. Gerry and Kate have devoted their lives to helping others. They are doing everything they can to get her back. They are staying in Portugal till that happens.'

This was the first intimation that, for the time being, the family was indeed going to make the little holiday resort their semi-permanent base. Kate clearly couldn't bear the idea of returning home without Maddy: it would be admitting that she might never get her child back.

But who had taken her? The latest suspects to emerge (though not named) were two German paedophiles, who lived about twenty miles away. There was a large German ex-pat community in the area, and a German child had gone missing five years previously and had never been found. Meanwhile the increasingly defensive Portuguese police were keen to emphasise that they were doing all they could: 'Portuguese officers are making a great effort,' said Armando Ferreira, president of the National Police Union. 'I have colleagues volunteering on their days off to help. Children disappear in England that are never found.' It was patently obvious that he was not happy that this had happened on his watch.

The McCanns saw the danger here: it was not in their interests to antagonise the local police. The couple made a point of expressing their gratitude to everyone who was involved in the hunt for their daughter: they made a point of praising the police. Even so, it did seem that the authorities had been a little blasé right from the start: a new lead emerged when a local shop owner said she had seen four men near the resort behaving suspiciously. They had been driving a car that had appeared both before and shortly after Maddy vanished. She had reported her concerns to the police, who had, apparently, told her they were too busy to follow up her concerns, and asked her to reappear the following morning.

And initially it seemed as if there might have been something in it. The car was first seen at the beginning of the week that Maddy went missing, near to the Marina Lagos. It was then seen again on the very night Maddy vanished between 10.30pm and 11.00pm: in the event, however, the story seemed to come to nothing.

There was also another possible sighting on CCTV cameras close to Praia da Luz. A woman had been seen at a petrol station with a child who fitted Maddy's description: she seemed to be urging the (very reluctant) child to say thank you to staff. What was of particular concern here was that the Galp service station was the first stop on the A22 motor-way, which cuts across the Algarve on the way to Spain. Under an open border principle known as the Schengen Agreement, there were no border controls between the two countries, which means no passports were required.

The McCanns resolutely refused to give up hope. They released a new statement: 'At present, we are channeling all of our emotions and all of our efforts into the steps that are being taken to secure Madeleine's safe return. We continue to remain positive.' Their fortitude was remarkable.

Inexplicably, given the amount of interest in the case from around the world and also, given the criticisms made towards the Portuguese police, less than a week after Maddy went missing, those self-same police announced they were scaling down the search. Searches of the local area had been 'initiated as soon as the disappearance was reported,' according to the police spokesman, Chief Inspector Olegario Sousa, but were now 'coming to an end. All places have been checked. The results are zero.' But, he added, the po-lice would continue to look for the little girl. 'We are pur-suing lines of investigation,' he said, amidst speculation that the police now believed Maddy was being held some-where else in Portugal or in another country. 'It was a de-cision of the officer in charge of the case. So I think they have changed something.' As to where the police believed

Maddy was being held: 'I will not speculate on this,' he said.

Another red herring cropped up with yet more CCTV footage, this time of three suspects in a car, one a woman, with a girl who looked like Maddy. They were seen by Nuno Lourenco, a Portuguese national now based in Germany, who said the gang had tried to kidnap his own daughter a few weeks previously, before he chased them off. Mr Lourenco, who, with his German wife, had two children aged two and four, had taken a photograph of them on his mobile phone: the McCanns, meanwhile, were whisked off to see the CCTV footage. The registration number of the car was circulated to Interpol and the British police. But like all the early sightings and leads, this one came to nought.

Even if the Portuguese police had scaled down the size of the local search, much was still going on in the background. Bill Henderson, the British Consul in the Algarve, was seen with the McCanns at the police station: the family themselves were pulling out all the stops to keep their daughter in the news. Indeed, in the coming weeks there would be a frenzy of publicity about the case, of a type rarely seen beforehand, that extended not just through Europe, but throughout the four corners of the globe. The family was to launch a campaign – run by professionals in a manner that was quite groundbreaking – with the aim of getting their daughter back. But of Maddy herself there was no trace.

The Ex-Pat Briton
with a Glass Eye

Nearly a week had passed since Madeleine went missing and everyone involved with the case was still at a complete loss. Early leads had come to nothing; although there were still mutterings about suspects, no one had been named as yet. The situation was looking increasingly grim. Detective Superintendant Albert Kirby, now retired, was brought in. He had been involved in the tragic case of James Bulger years earlier, and was asked by the Portuguese police to help. 'The police asked for the opportunity to speak to me directly and I was able to discuss with them aspects of the Bulger case and others I have been involved in,' he said. 'It is almost a week since she has been taken and we all have serious concerns about her well being.' So did much of the world.

By the time Madeleine had been missing for a week, others – who had nothing to do with the police – were stepping in to help. The McCanns themselves were offering a £100,000 reward if their daughter was returned. The *Daily Express* reported that Don Holmes, a British businessman who runs an Algarve-based construction company, put up a further reward of £7,000. A bigger sum still was offered: £1 million by Stephen Winyard, a businessman and father-of-three: this was, however, rejected by the Portuguese police on the grounds that they could not accept cash as it might prejudice the investigation. Portuguese law certainly seemed to be offering more problems than it solved.

It had been a terrible week for Maddy's parents. As well as having to cope with the fact that their daughter had gone missing, Kate and Gerry had been spending hours and hours at a time in the police headquarters in Portimao. They had to study, amongst much else, pictures of local paedophiles in order to determine whether they'd been seen in the area, as well as looking at endless reels of CCTV footage. Kate had to endure one nine-hour stretch there. Gerry, meanwhile, spent up to fourteen hours at a time.

The strain was telling on both of them, but still they bore up. 'We have now seen at first hand how hard the police are working in the search for Madeleine and their strong desire to find her,' Gerry said. 'We are doing absolutely everything to assist police with their investigation and will leave no stone unturned in the search for our daughter. We have been moved by the enormous willingness of people to do all they can to help find Madeleine.'

Amidst much publicity, the police picked up two men

and a woman, dressed in bathing costumes, on the nearby beach, and took them for questioning. It came to nothing. It was reported that the family had been in the nearby town of Sagres on the day someone was taking photographs of little blonde girls: again, the lead dried up almost as soon as it surfaced. The police briefly detained a British couple: they, too, were found to have no involvement with the case. The mystery grew.

One week to the day after Maddy vanished was made even worse by the fact that it was her fourth birthday, and the family had been planning to celebrate it at home. A party had been planned with dozens of friends, and a Dr Who birthday cake – it was Maddy's favourite programme. Instead, of course, the family was stuck in Spain.

The inhabitants of Rothley, the village in which the McCanns lived, wanted to do something to show their solidarity with the family, and their sorrow at what had happened, and so to mark the event, balloons were released at nearby Queniborough Hall. One carried a note that read, 'Mummy and Daddy, Sean and Amelie – we'll see you soon.'

In Praia da Luz, a special Mass was held at the village church to mark Maddy's birthday. The front two rows of the church were lined with family and friends, and Gerry addressed the congregation. 'Today we should be celebrating the fourth birthday of our daughter Madeleine,' he said. 'Instead we have to remember what a normal, beautiful, vivacious, funny, courageous and loving little girl we are missing today. I like to think about the effects of Madeleine's abduction from us nine days ago as like a tidal wave. The devastation, which was tremendous, was greatest for Kate and I. [But] the devastation affects everyone we meet here in the resort and has affected this community.

'The tidal wave did not stop here: it has travelled many miles across Europe, across the sea to Glasgow, Liverpool, Leicester, Ireland, America, Canada, New Zealand and continental Europe, where we have many friends and family. The devastation might not be quite as great, but this tidal wave is still wreaking havoc. We got tremendous support immediately from our friends and we prayed, of course, we prayed. We prayed for Madeleine, we prayed for ourselves. When we came to the church on Sunday there was the most tremendous outpouring of warmth and support, which lifted us in addition. That strength, hope and courage which was given to us, we have spoken to other people, and we have told them of our hope and how we look forward to this joyous day and this has helped everyone around us remain strong – as we seem to everyone around.'

Gerry also mentioned the vigils taking place back in Britain. 'They have taken our strength and they are taking action, these actions are to make Madeleine's disappearance more public in the hope that we will get her back sooner as a result. This has also given us great strength that we are doing everything in our power to get Madeleine back. We walked out of this church [the previous week] believing that we will see Madeleine soon and she will be safe and well and we will continue to hope. And above all, we thank all of you for giving us strength to believe that and for the messages from around Portugal, Spain, Britain, Europe and the world give us that strength. Thank you.'

The congregation was greatly moved: they burst out into spontaneous applause. Many were carrying gifts for Madeleine; all were wearing yellow string around their wrists, tied there by the children of the village. Gerry McCann smiled and even laughed as the villagers held their presents aloft and, for the first time since the saga began, Kate managed a smile.

And the family were certainly resolute. 'We are looking forward to the day when Madeleine returns to us as a joyous one,' said Gerry, as the family emerged from the steps of the church. 'We walked out of this church believing we will see Madeleine soon and she will be safe and well and we will continue to hope.'

Birthday cards were also left at the war memorial in the McCann's village back in Britain. 'People in the village would like to mark Madeleine's birthday, but felt it was inappropriate to turn it into a party atmosphere,' said Valerie Armstrong, a pub landlady who had organised the vigil. 'The family felt it would be better to wait for Madeleine to come home and have a party and a cake then.' Meanwhile, well wishers continued to put yellow ribbons, messages of support and cuddly toys on the war memorial: 'The village green here is continuing to be a focal point, not just for those in this village, but all other villages,' Mrs Armstrong explained. Back in Portugal, the McCanns attended a vigil in church. David Beckham became the latest star to appeal for Maddy's return.

Despite the efforts of the Portuguese police, the reward for Maddy now stood at £2.5 million, with businessmen including Virgin's Sir Richard Branson and retail billionaire Sir Philip Green making contributions to the fund; the family used the day to issue another appeal. 'On Madeleine's birthday, please keep looking, please keep praying, please help bring Madeleine home,' they said in a statement. 'We would like to mark today by asking people to redouble their efforts. We know there is already a huge amount of effort and resources being put into the search for our daughter. We also know that offers of support are made daily. It is this that keeps us strong and gives us hope.'

In other parts of Britain, there were also ceremonies

for the little girl. In Glasgow, Maddy's uncle John McCann held a vigil for her, lighting four candles on a cake and singing Happy Birthday, before praying for her safe return. In Liverpool, Madeleine's grandmother Susan Healy wept as she said, 'We just have to keep praying.' Their grief was palpable and felt by the nation, too.

One person who really did know how the family was feeling is Anita B (her surname can not be made public for legal reasons), who comes from Bergheim-Elsdorf, near Cologne, the mother of a six-year-old boy, Rene, who had been snatched eleven years previously from a beach twenty miles from where the McCanns were staying, and who hadn't been seen since. The child had been walking just twenty yards behind his parents, who, every year since then, return to the Algarve in the hope of finding him. 'We know what you are going through and how painful it must be,' she said.

Various theories were now emerging. There were rumblings when it turned out that the number plates on the suspicious looking van were false. One of the men in the van resembled someone the Spanish police were hunting in the wake of the attempted rape of a ten-year-old girl. There were also fears that Madeleine had been targeted even before the family left Britain, but it was all wild speculation: no one knew for sure.

There was one positive development: the campaign to find Maddy was really gaining pace. Everyone seemed to want to help, whether they were neighbours of the family or had never even met the McCanns. In Glasgow, Maddy's aunt Diane McCann took part in a ten-kilometre road race in which she and thousands of other cyclists wore t-shirts with Maddy's picture on them and yellow ribbons. 'We're hoping to show solidarity for the family and show everyone we are rooting for Madeleine to come home as soon as possible,' she said.

Elsewhere, other events were also taking place. At Chelsea's Stamford Bridge ground, fans of Everton, which was Maddy's favourite football team, wore the t-shirts, as did Everton captain Phil Neville before kick-off. Across Portugal, people were leaving presents and pictures of Maddy, and yellow ribbons were tied to railings in an effort to highlight the family's plight. The reward money had risen to £2.6 million, and a trust was established as a fighting fund for the McCanns, as donations poured in from across the world. It was to provide financial support for the family and pay any rewards or legal bills they might incur as they fought on to 'leave no stone unturned.'

One way in which the family was attempting to draw attention to Maddy was by a new poster campaign, showing pictures of the little girl with the caption, 'Look into my eyes!'

It highlighted a distinctive 'black flash' in Maddy's right eye, in which her pupil ran into her blue green iris, something that a kidnapper, had he tried to change her appearance, would have found impossible to disguise. 'Please look, at children, don't be afraid, look for this black flash that goes from her pupil to the iris of her eye,' Maddy's grandmother Susan Healy, who described her as her 'bright, shining star', begged. 'If those who have got Madeleine realise she has this distinctive marking, take her somewhere safe. Leave her, you can run off, we don't care. We just want Madeleine back.' The poster was important: there were now concerns that a kidnapper might have tried to disguise Maddy's appearance by cutting her hair or dyeing it black.

The latest theory to emerge was that Maddy had been chloroformed, which is why the people who took her had managed to get away so quietly. There had been no signs of disturbance at the scene, and so they were now asking local chemists if they had recently sold any insect sprays containing chloroform or any other knock out drug. Anyone who had been buying travel sickness pills for children was also being looked out for.

Kate and Gerry, looking utterly shattered, marked the eleventh day of their daughter's disappearance by walking hand-in-hand along the beach. Kate was carrying Maddy's Cuddle Cat toy, as she had done almost constantly since the dreadful saga began: the two sat sadly on the rocks, looking out to sea, before returning to the apartment once more. Later, Kate went to church where, again, prayers for Maddy were said.

It was at around this time that rumours first surfaced about an actual suspect the police had in mind. A source within the Portuguese police had said, 'We have not questioned any suspects and we do not have any suspects in mind,' but increasingly one name was beginning to do the rounds. The identity of the man had not yet been made public, but it was believed that he was a fellow Brit, who lived on the edge of the Ocean Club complex. He was believed to have been one of ten people questioned by the police in the wake of Maddy's disappearance and, under Portuguese law, he was going to be asked to swear a witness statement to a magistrate. The McCanns were going to be able to be present and put forward questions. At last, it seemed as if the police were really onto something. It was nearly two weeks now since Maddy vanished and this seemed to be the first concrete lead.

In a separate development, two British lawyers from the International Family Law Group had flown into Portugal to advise the family on what to do next. The local search had been called off – despite the fact that the McCanns were desperate for it to continue – with the police adamant that

Maddy could no longer be anywhere nearby (this would also seem to counter later allegations made against the parents). The McCanns were also resigned to a lengthy stay in Portugal, and needed help in the mountain of paperwork that had built up: they needed to verify witness statements before the magistrate to complete the formal legal process. It was wearisome detail in the face of tragedy, but it had to be done.

'We have brought in our lawyers to help us decide how to best use these offers of support to help us find Madeleine,' said Gerry. 'Since the lawyers have come here we have felt a burden being lifted from our shoulders because it is one less thing we do not have to immediately think about. This has allowed us to concentrate more on our own physical and mental well being.'

In their continuing efforts to keep the story in the spotlight, Kate and Gerry gave another interview to talk about their plight. Kate revealed that the family intended to stay in Portugal for the foreseeable future: 'We can't even consider going home for the moment,' she said. 'I absolutely can't even let it enter my head.'

The past couple of weeks had, unsurprisingly, been taking its toll. Kate had been having trouble eating and sleeping, but said that she and Gerry had gained strength from the astonishing amount of support being shown from around the world, and wanted to take up regular regimes such as jogging again.

And the couple remained resolutely optimistic. 'As far as we are concerned, until there is concrete evidence to the contrary, we believe Madeleine is safe and being looked after,' Gerry said. 'We need to keep Madeleine's profile high. This is essential in the search for Madeleine. We are fully supporting the investigation. We have brought in the lawyers to advise us what else can be done. I don't know what that is at the moment.'

Indeed, while the couple remained extremely supportive of the Portuguese police, behind the scenes they were looking at others ways to move forward. The fact was that the official investigation had produced nothing to date, and so clearly other measures needed to be taken. 'Kate and Gerry and other members of the family are very resourceful and are coming up with lots of ideas about what can be done,' said a source close to the family. 'They won't do anything to get in the way of the Portuguese police investigation, but want to do whatever they can to move forward.'

Back in England, however, there was growing criticism of the Portuguese police. Writing in the *Sunday Express*, John Stalker, the ex-deputy chief constable of Greater Manchester Police, was scathing about the way the case had been handled, comparing it to the popular television programme *Life On Mars*, in which a modern police officer finds himself in the altogether less professional world of the 1970s.

'British police ... can never be accused of complacency when a three-year-old child is reported missing,' he wrote. 'In these cases, they hit the ground running – which never happened in Portugal. From the first moment Madeleine went missing, the Portuguese police moved too slowly. The feeling seems to have been that child abductions simply do not happen on the Algarve and a benign explanation would soon emerge. They were tragically wrong. Local police dealt with the inquiry during those precious first few hours when fast-moving investigations such as these are won or lost. The National CID belatedly moved in to take over but clues had been lost.'

Meanwhile, there had been further developments in a different area. It was becoming an open secret that the police had an actual suspect in mind and now, for the first time, his name was made public: Robert Murat. A flood of details emerged. He was a stocky man, with a glass eye, which school friends revealed he used to pop out of its socket as a party trick. Murat, 33, had been living in Portugal for sixteen years, after his English mother and Portuguese father moved to the country: he was currently locked in a custody battle with his estranged wife Dawn, who lived in

Norfolk, over their four-year-old daughter Sofia. Much was made about this in the weeks to come, not least because Murat pointed out the resemblance between his own child and Madeleine.

In some eyes, at least, Murat had been acting suspiciously. He lived in Casa Liliana with his mother Jennifer, 71, in a villa just one hundred yards from the McCanns, and had seemed to appoint himself as an unofficial go-between between the family and the police. He had volunteered to help translate witness statements by English holidaymakers and, although he was an estate agent, appeared to some people to be a little vague about what he actually did. It was journalists in the vicinity who first raised doubts about him, not least because his behaviour was slightly reminiscent of Ian Huntley, the Soham murderer, who had also volunteered to help the police before his crime was revealed. That said, volunteering to help the police is not actually a crime.

Eyebrows were further raised when he commented, 'I know how it feels to Madeleine's parents, because I have a daughter aged three-and-a-half who I am in a custody battle over.' Of course, his daughter had not actually disappeared, leading to some comment that his remarks were at best tactless, and at worst – who knew?

It was one reporter in particular, Lori Campbell, who first voiced reservations about Murat. She had a 'gut feeling' about him. 'From the beginning he was on the scene from day one,' she said. 'He was always talking to the media and giving his opinion about what was going on. When I asked what he did, he was very vague but seemed to be acting as if he was an official. But after a few days he admitted he was just a local guy.'

From the moment his name was made public, matters moved fast. The police named him as a suspect and brought him in for questioning, although he was not placed under arrest. It turned out that he had made extremely unwise remarks to reporters about being a prime suspect in the investigation (he was joking, apparently), and further, after being asked about his role in the investigation, had become jumpy and vanished for four days. It was believed that he had, in fact, gone to England, where the battle with his estranged wife continued.

Certainly, neighbours in the village in west Norfolk, in which he had lived, expressed bewilderment when he was named as a suspect in the case. 'He is a perfect man to my mind,' said one. 'I see no reason to say that he is unfriendly. He is a lovely man. He was really proud of his little girl. His ex-wife is a wonderful girl, too.'

Back in Portugal, Murat's mother Jennifer, an ex-nurse who had also been amongst the first to join the search for Madeleine, was visibly distressed by the turn of events. Her son was innocent, she said, and had been with her on the night that Madeleine disappeared. Nonetheless, the villa was being subjected to minute scrutiny: tarpaulins covered the building, and a water tank near the swimming pool was examined. Forensic experts were swarming all over the villa and sniffer dogs had been brought in. The patio was dug up, soil samples were taken and a thorough investigation of a shed and car was carried out. Murat's uncle ran a bar in nearby Burgau: that, too, was searched.

It was Lori Campbell, again, who voiced the concerns that had been raised. 'Basically, he surfaced on Friday afternoon last week, and was walking around as if he was someone official,' she said. 'He claimed that he was just a local guy who spoke fluent Portuguese and English and was helping the family. He was coming in and out of the family apartment, speaking with the media. But when questioned about it, he was very vague. He said he just volunteered to help the police with their investigation. He was in and out of the apartment throughout the week. He said he was just helping to translate witness statements. He said he was from the UK, going through a divorce back there. He was angry about the way the British media had criticised Portuguese police over their handling of the investigation. He was coming up with lots of suggestions about what had happened to Madeleine and said he thought she had probably been taken to Spain.'

It must be said that none of this actually constituted a crime. But the case was so strange, with no leads that had come to anything concrete, that a certain amount of grasping at straws was going on, simply because people were so desperate to discover exactly what had happened.

Just as the McCanns' relatives had leapt to their defence, though, so Robert Murat's family and friends came out for him. Catherine Roberts, a friend of the family, expressed her bewilderment. 'He has been repeatedly stopped and questioned by the police over the last few days because his daughter looks so much like Madeleine,' she said. 'I can't believe this has happened. They are a lovely family.'

His aunt, Sally Eveleigh, who runs a guesthouse in Lagos, near Praia da Luz, was similarly bemused. There was 'absolutely no way' he could be involved in Madeleine's disappearance, she said, adding that his own daughter's resemblance to Maddy was not exactly grounds for an arrest. Quite a few other children did, too. 'Are we going to accuse all fathers of all these children of that?' she asked. 'They [the police] had heard from English reporters that this was happening, that Robert had said he missed his daughter so much. And from that, because they've got nothing to go on, they all started assuming. I've known him all his life and there's absolutely no way. He loves children, but not to something like that.'

Indeed, just about everyone who knew him was shocked by the allegations. Gaynor de Jesus, who had been at school with Murat, and had been translating for news organisations, was similarly taken aback. 'He was a quiet guy and very friendly,' he said. 'His mum has helped running a stall at the scene trying to get information about the missing girl. She had taken it upon herself to gather information regarding the case for the police if local people or holidaymakers felt uncomfortable talking to officers. I was quite surprised by him saying he was an official translator for the police, because he did not speak Portuguese fluently. But the police seemed to confirm what he was saying is true.'

The furore about Murat was a welcome distraction for the police: at least it shifted the spotlight off an investigation that had so far found nothing. The British consul, John Buck, a diplomat to the hilt, continued to praise them: 'impressive resources' had been dedicated to finding Madeleine, he said. The collaboration between the British and Portuguese police was 'truly exceptional.' As for the McCanns, they were showing, 'remarkable resilience and dignity in very distressing circumstances.' That, certainly, was true.

Mr Buck had spoken to the national chief of police in Lisbon and the chief investigating officer in the Algarve: 'There are clearly impressive resources being devoted to this investigation,' he continued. 'Those resources are, rightly, primarily Portuguese, but we also have a number of British police officers working closely with their Portuguese colleagues here in the Algarve.' As far as the McCanns were concerned, he thanked the media on their behalf. 'They appreciate that the media have an important role to play in finding Madeleine,' he said. 'They and I are very grateful for the constructive, responsible and considerate way in which the media have approached this.'

Until now, Robert Murat himself had been silent. But as the search for Maddy edged towards its third week, he clearly felt it was time to speak. The police had removed mobile phones, computers and clothing from his home and put him under surveillance. They had neither arrested nor charged him, although one Portuguese newspaper reported that paedophile sites had been found on the computer. 'This has ruined my life and it's made things very difficult here and in Britain,' he said. 'The only way I will survive this is if they catch Madeleine's abductors. I have been made a scapegoat for something I didn't do.'

It was certainly the case, though, that his behaviour had been very odd. *Daily Express* reporter Matt Drake was another who saw Murat at close quarters: 'Every time I saw him on that first morning after Madeleine's disappearance, he never moved more than twenty yards from where she had been snatched,' he revealed. 'He told me he was an official translator between the police and the family. But not once during those desperate hours did I see him speak to police officers at the scene or act with any authority. Instead, he stood, watched and spoke mainly to females about why he alone wanted to find Madeleine more than anyone else.'

Murat then made matters worse by constantly harping on about his own daughter. 'He told me how his own daughter was the "spitting image" of the four year old,' Drake continued. 'It was the kind of comment that strikes a chord and I discretely motioned a nearby photographer to capture his picture, should it be needed later. He said he was tired after hours of searching and his back ached with the strain.'

Murat, it seemed, had been clutching a picture of Maddy throughout the investigation, and continued that after so many years of living in Portugal, he did not believe a paedophile could have taken her in 'his country.' Of his own child he said, 'I only wish I could be with her.'

His behaviour grew odder still. 'As I grew more curious about this strange man, I asked his name and age, but he said he could be quoted only as Bob and preferred to keep his surname and age private,' said Drake. 'I explained my fears to colleagues, but they joked and said it was only because with his tinted glasses and dead glass eye, he fitted the profile of "child snatcher."'

It had certainly been a horrible experience for Murat (and one that was far from over). He had telephoned his mother telling her, 'I am innocent. I am very upset and I think that the Portuguese police are just trying to find an Englishman to blame.' He was 'totally devastated' he said to Sally Eveleigh. 'Robert is shattered by this,' Mrs Eveleigh continued. 'He feels his life has been ruined forever. He offered his help as a translator to police and Madeleine's parents through pure goodwill. Now this has all been turned against him and he is devastated.'

A spokesman for the Murat family added, 'They are elated he has been released. The police had to let him go because they have got no evidence on him.' But it was a very bizarre episode and one that was to run on and on.

Madeleine's case was now beginning to have far reaching implications. There was a call for a crackdown on the free movement of convicted paedophiles throughout the EU by the Scottish MEP Struan Stevenson, who revealed that over one hundred paedophiles who were listed on the sex offenders register in the UK had travelled to and from Portugal that year. 'The tragic case of Madeleine McCann has highlighted the ludicrous loopholes in legislation covering the movement of convicted paedophiles,' he said, adding that he was 'horrified' when he discovered how many had travelled between Britain and Portugal. 'No attempt was made by the UK authorities to notify their opposite numbers in Portugal as to the identity of these dangerous predators until after the kidnapping of Madeleine came to light,' he said. 'I assume that thousands may be travelling at any time throughout the EU. I have therefore written to Franco Frattini [the EU Commissioner for Justice, Freedom and Security] asking him to consider a regulation which will force EU member states to share information.' The EU should ban all travel by the most serious offenders, he said, including paedophiles.

Back in Portugal, the focus was still on Robert Murat. Although he had been released, the Portuguese police were far from signalling that he was in the clear: he was still a 'formal suspect' and when Chief Inspector Olegario Sousa was asked if charges might yet be brought against him, he replied, 'Let's wait and see. We are hopeful that this case will be over in the near future.'

More details began to emerge about police searches. Murat ran his estate agency business with his 30-something married German lover Michaela Wulczuch: the police had begun searching the business premises, especially those in remote locations. They also searched the flat Ms Wulczuch shared with her Portuguese husband Luis Antonio. 'Five searches were conducted,' said Chief Inspector Sousa. 'The main purpose was to collect information allowing us to bring back and locate young Madeleine.' As to why Murat had been released: 'We are not saying there is no evidence against this man, we are just saying there is not enough,' Sousa said. On the advice of his mother, Murat went into hiding and this strange case moved on.

A Tidal Wave of Hope

It was nearly three weeks now since Madeleine had disappeared, but her family was determined not to give up. The appeal had spread to Westminster: as a fund was launched to help the hunt, some of Madeleine's relatives met the then-chancellor Gordon Brown, alongside the then-deputy prime minister, John Prescott. It was a day of good cheer.

'Instead of a tidal wave of despair, my brother Gerry is facing a tidal wave of hope,' said Philomena McCann, speaking outside Westminster. 'Initially he was completely floored by what had happened and found it very difficult to cope. That was turned around by the support of the nation of Portugal, the support of Glasgow, the whole of Scotland and England. Madeleine is a beautiful, caring little girl. I can quite understand why someone might take her – but give her back. She is not yours.' Of the meeting with Gordon Brown, she said, 'He was very distressed about our situation. I felt he was a genuine and caring person; I was touched by his sensitivity.'

Meanwhile in Leicester, Madeleine's uncle John McCann

and her grandparents Brian and Susan Healy were unveiling at Walkers Stadium details of the new fund. Amongst those in attendance was the former England and Leicester Tigers rugby player Martin Johnson. 'This story has touched everyone, but as a father it really does hit home,' he said. 'I am here to lend any support I can.'

Back in Portugal, matters were still on the move. The Portuguese police were now quizzing a Russian computer expert, believed to be Moscow-born Sergey Malinka, 22, who had set up a website for Robert Murat's property company Romigen. Police cars were seen outside his flat, while Malinka was taken in for questioning.

The reason he had come to the attention of the police in the first place was that a conversation he'd had with Robert Murat was captured on a mobile phone. And, as with Murat himself, those who knew him expressed astonishment. He was a 'sweet kid' who 'fixed everybody's computers,' according to Tuck Price, a friend of the Murats. 'He set up Robert's website,' he continued. 'Why they're searching him I don't know, but it's still distressing to Robert. All that is pointing out that they're not looking elsewhere.'

Malinka himself was bemused by it all. Before he was taken in for questioning, he'd been told that detectives were looking for a Russian man with a criminal record for violence: 'I don't know whom they mean,' he said. 'It's definitely not me. I have just had all my residency papers approved and checks are always made for criminal convictions. I have done nothing wrong. I did some work for Robert and found him a really cool guy. He wanted a website created and I did a lot of work putting it together.'

Murat himself continued to be very distressed about the turn of events. 'Robert is in pieces over what has happened,' said his uncle, Ralph Everleigh, 62. 'He can't believe it and has been struggling to cope with this intrusion into his life. He spoke to his ex-wife today back in England and she is in a terrible mess and very annoyed by what has happened to Robert. She told him that she never believed he was capable of doing what they said he had. He is so angry that he cannot tell his side, but here in Portugal the law is very strict regarding that sort of thing. His mum has had to sign an oath for police, so now she can't speak about what has happened. Their house is ruined – they have dug things up and knocked down walls but it was all for nothing in the end. They have stopped searching now and it looks like they believe Robert is innocent and was with his mum on the night the little girl went missing.'

But whatever the police believed – and it sometimes seemed to change within the hour – there was one problem: they didn't have any other suspect. A slightly less complementary picture of Malinka was also in evidence, when two of his former colleagues spoke out. One said that he had boasted of having sex with a girl of fourteen; another, from a different firm, said she had found him downloading pornography.

'It was top shelf stuff, boys' stuff, blue movies,' she said. 'I didn't mention it to him. He is very clever with computers and knows everything there is to know about them. He wants to earn big money, but doesn't want to put the work in.'

The other former colleague was more caustic still. 'Every week he would go through Praia da Luz with very young girlfriends,' she said. 'The last one was fourteen years old. It was the straw that broke the camel's back. It was around two years ago I saw this and told the police what I knew. I ran to one of the police posts last Wednesday afternoon to tell them what I knew.'

Malinka himself was livid about allegations as to what had been found on his computer. 'The Portuguese press said they found some paedophile content on my computer,' he fumed. 'That is a lie. Nothing has been found. My equipment has been released and returned to me. I'm trying to help in any way possible.'

Meanwhile, there was a possible sighting of Maddy in Lisbon: the police said they were searching for a red van with fake number plates in a southern suburb of the city. A witness had seen a child who fitted Maddy's description

– but this lead, like all the others, came to nothing. Another theory was that she'd been smuggled to Africa and sold to child traffickers after a woman claimed to have seen a small child with a suspicious-looking man in Marrakech. The child was said to be looking sad and asking, 'Can I see my mummy now' – but, of course, there might have been a perfectly innocent explanation.

The person who made the sighting was Norwegian-born Mari Pollard, now resident in southern Spain, who had seen the two outside the Ibis Palmeraie Hotel outside Marrakech. The man, who was white with brown hair, seemed to be aged between thirty-five and forty, and the child, according to Mrs Pollard, was 'a sweet blonde-haired girl with a very cute face. She was wearing blue pyjamas with a little pink and white pattern on her top.' When she saw the child, Mrs Pollard had been unaware of the hunt for Madeleine: it was only when she returned home to Spain that she made a connection. 'When I saw the picture, I knew the girl I had seen was Madeleine,' she said. 'I feel I should have done something. She looked so sad and alone.' Mrs Pollard and her husband Ray notified the authorities but, as with so many of the alleged sightings, it ultimately came to nought.

The rumours swirling around Murat refused to go away. It was reported that although he'd said he hadn't spoken to

Malinka in months, there was evidence of telephone calls between the two of them shortly after Madeleine went missing: one a mere thirty minutes after Madeleine vanished and then several more over the next two hours.

It was also hinted that he'd asked several different people to give him an alibi for the night in question. 'Murat made and received calls on his mother's mobile,' said one of the local papers. 'Calls were also made from the landline at the Englishman's house. The Russian couldn't explain the calls.' The two had also been captured speaking together on CCTV cameras. The police made their feelings clear: 'This is one more incident that led to suspicions falling on him,' said a source.

Matters seemed to get even worse when it emerged that Malinka might not even have been in the country legally. The Russian embassy in Lisbon had no record of him; he was also linked to a firm in Lagos offering trips to north Africa. But, of course, none of this was actual proof that he'd had anything whatsoever to do with Maddy; nor that Murat did, either. Indeed, Murat's estranged wife made a point of saying she 'sincerely' believed her husband to be innocent. His girlfriend Michaela stuck up for him, too: 'He had nothing to do with this,' she said. 'He was only trying to help out and find the little girl. He has been treated terribly and doesn't know why.'

He didn't help himself when he refused to take a lie detector test. According to his family, there would have been no point. 'It would not make any difference,' said his aunt, Sally Eveleigh. 'He says he is innocent and anything he does will only make things worse. He says it would not make any difference at all as it is not legal here in Portugal. Robert is certain it would not help his case. Not that he has any case to answer.'

He did, though, concede there was a link with Malinka, who had reportedly phoned Murat's landline half an hour after Madeleine had gone missing. When there was no answer, he apparently called Murat's mother Jennifer. 'Robert did meet with Sergey,' Sally Eveleigh confirmed. 'He is just not certain which day it was. He does not remember speaking to Sergey on the phone on the night the little girl vanished.' Shortly afterwards there was a renewed outcry at the actions of the Portuguese police, who had allowed Murat to stroll in and out of the McCann's holiday apartment almost at will, thus totally nullifying any DNA evidence that might have been there.

An order of Carmelite nuns from northern Portugal were the next to offer as much support as they could: they sent emails across the country asking people to pause and pray for ten minutes on the Portuguese feast of hope. Madeleine had been missing for two and a half weeks when her parents clearly felt they could not just sit around waiting to hear about sightings that came to nothing. The Find Madeleine Fund had been officially launched and Gerry started on what was to be the first of many trips around the globe in the search for his daughter, when he flew back to Britain to consult lawyers and advisors on how best to proceed. It was the first time the family would be separated since it all began; meanwhile both McCanns were on indefinite leave from work. They would leave 'no stone unturned' in the attempt to find their daughter, they said; nor did they want to leave Portugal without her. Support in Portugal and across the world was as strong for the family as ever: on 21 May, the nation observed a minute of silence at noon to focus on attempts to recover the child.

Relatives of the McCanns remained as supportive as ever. 'For now they don't talk about leaving Praia da Luz,' Madeleine's great-uncle Brian Kennedy explained. 'When I spoke to Gerry, he said if it was necessary they would use some of the money from the fund to go around the world and tell the story of Madeleine. They would go personally to places raising awareness. Not finding Madeleine is not an option.'

There was also a suggestion that the McCanns might hire a private detective, although, with its implication that the Portuguese police were not up to the job, this was a subject that had to be handled delicately. 'We've already spoken several times about this to Gerry,' Brian continued. 'It is not something that has been decided yet. Maybe at some point down the road it will happen but, for now, there is a respect for the Portuguese authorities. But it has been a long time. It's already too much for all of us. My wife wakes up many times each night and calls for Madeleine.'

The Foreign Office was also being extremely supportive of the McCanns. A spokeswoman had been assigned to liaise with them and she reported, 'They are taking advice on what is right. If it means going around Europe to meet people, talk to people, then they will do it. They haven't sat down and drawn up any plans, but it is where their thoughts are going at the moment.'

It was, in a way, inevitable that the überguru of controversial PR, Max Clifford, would become involved at some stage of the proceedings and that moment had now arrived. The McCanns scarcely needed more positive publicity than they were already getting, but the Murats certainly did, and so it was Robert and his mother Jennifer who gave Max a call. Clifford himself said he felt 'a tremendous amount of sympathy' for Murat, but that he would not officially represent him until the police had cleared him. 'When I spoke to Robert, he was in tears, and said, "I am innocent and I will prove I am innocent," and thanked me for listening to him,' he said. 'I told him that provided he is cleared, I will be happy to talk to him because everyone in the world will want to interview him.'

And would he seek payment for any future interview? Tuck Price stepped in. 'Robert's concern is to clear his name,' he said. 'After that, things may change.'

As events moved on, the McCanns had to do something they must have been dreading: ask Sean and Amelie if they could remember anything about the night of 3 May. The twins were completely unaware of what had been going on around them: their parents had managed to get them to see it as an extended holiday. They still had no idea Madeleine had disappeared and that a worldwide hunt was on. And although Gerry and Kate felt they had to be questioned, it was done in such a way that they still didn't realise what was happening.

With the police now openly beginning to voice doubts as to whether Maddy would be found alive, the McCanns refused to give up hope. And support still flooded in. David Beckham and Helen Mirren headed up the Greatest Britons 2007 awards in London: they and everyone else wore yellow ribbons to mark the day. The *James Bond* star Daniel Craig was also wearing a yellow ribbon at the Cannes film festival. Gerry urged anyone who had any photographs at all of anyone who could possibly be Madeleine to send them to a special website.

After his brief visit to Britain, Gerry was now back in Portugal with Kate and the twins, something that was clearly a relief. 'It was extremely difficult to leave here without Kate,' he said, as he stood holding his wife's hand near to the apartment where Madeleine had vanished. 'When I went into Rothley, I knew we should have been coming home as a family of five.'

'It was moving for me to see Gerry in Rothley,' said Kate. 'It emphasised how much support we have got there and everywhere. It really helps. Gerry told me about the overwhelming support he received during his visit home. The love and messages he received are very moving. Both of us are very grateful for all the support. It gives us strength and keeps us focused on the positive."

Gerry chipped in again. 'We will travel wherever necessary to ensure people across Europe recognise Madeleine's picture and encourage them to come forward with information,' he said. 'Both of us have taken a great deal of strength from our faiths. We want to visit the shrine at Fatima to pray for Madeleine's return to us.' And of the money in the fund he continued, 'There will be significant legal expenses as a legal team has come in to advise us. That has lifted a great burden from our shoulders. And we will fund the website, which is a great vehicle for information regarding Madeleine's disappearance.'

And for now, at least, the family had decided not to hire a private detective. 'The thrust of the investigation will be that being run by the Portuguese with the assistance of the British police,' he said. Our family strongly believes that somebody in the public holds a piece of information. That is why we have campaigned so vigorously to make sure her disappearance is publicised as widely as possible. We don't know if Madeleine is in Portugal. We have to consider the possibility she has crossed borders. We are spreading the net far and wide. We are hopeful that the latest appeal will lead to key information, whether it comes from Portugal, the UK or farther afield. We are concentrating on Continental Europe.'

He refused, however, to be drawn on the subject of Robert Murat. 'I hope everyone treats suspects the way we would hope to be treated,' he said. 'That is, presumed innocent until charged, arrested or convicted.'

There were already increasing numbers of pictures of Madeleine in the public domain, and to mark the three-week anniversary of her disappearance, another was released, one that had been taken on the afternoon of 3 May. It was a delightful picture, and showed a giggling Maddy in a pink top and white shorts, wearing a sun hat to prevent her from the sun. It was an enchanting sight, but one that betrayed an increasing anxiety on the part of her parents for, three weeks on, no one really had any clue whatsoever as to what had happened.

Madeleine's uncle John McCann spoke for the whole family when he said as much. 'Obviously while Madeleine is still not back, we are very disappointed,' he said. 'We hope the authorities are going to explore more avenues and focus the resources very much on sightings and other information.'

A source close to the family was more abrupt. 'Kate and Gerry are getting increasingly frustrated,' he said. 'They are getting concerned at the slowness of the Portuguese investigation. They fully comprehend the restrictions the Portuguese legal system places on everyone, but naturally as parents who want their little girl back, some of the delays are frustrating. The British police have been great, but even they are not in the loop. They are considering how they can move things forward themselves. They want to do positive things in their search for Madeleine.'

Of course, alongside all the messages of support, there had been the critics, who right from the start slammed the McCanns as being responsible for their plight. After all, there were various different types of baby sitting and crèche facilities on offer and they hadn't used any of them. It was dreadfully upsetting for the family, not least because the events of the previous three weeks were very clearly taking their toll. Both looked strained and exhausted. And as they themselves said, no one could blame them more than they did themselves.

'The guilt will never leave us,' said Gerry in a sombre interview. 'Many people say to us that this is a parent's worst nightmare, and it is.'

'I think at worst we were naïve,' said Kate, who was clutching Maddy's Cuddle Cat. 'We are very responsible parents. We love our children very much. I don't think any parent could ever imagine something like this happening. I can't think about leaving, I can't think about going home without Madeleine. I think every parent will know that feeling [of panic and despair when Maddy disappeared.] I think people are aware we were checking regularly on the children and it was during one of my checks that I discovered she had gone. I can't really go into details about it, but I'm sure any parent will realise how that felt. I panicked.'

But why didn't they use a babysitter? Gerry stepped into the breach. 'I think if you know the location here, we have been reassured by the thousands of messages from people who have either done exactly the same or said they would have done the same. For us, it wasn't really very much different from having dinner in your garden, in the proximity of the location. I think it's fair to say the guilt we feel having not been there at that moment will never leave us. It's difficult to say if it's a lesson for other parents.

'We've tried to rationalise things in our head, but ultimately what's done is done. We have tried to look forward. If you think about the millions and millions of British families who go to the Mediterranean each year, really the chances of this happening are in the order of one hundred million to one. No one hurts you as much as the hurt that we had, but we have tried to remain very positive in our outlook and even small levels of criticism make that hard when you're trying to do everything in your power to get your daughter back. It's as bad as you can possibly imagine, but if all three of the children had been taken, it could have been even worse than your worst nightmare.' And the twins were actually a help. 'They're here and they do bring you back to earth,' Gerry went on. 'We cannot grieve – we did grieve, of course we grieve – but ultimately you need to be in control so that we can influence and help in any way possible.'

Kate spoke again. 'Certainly, the first few days, the guilt was very difficult, but as time goes on we feel stronger and we felt very supported,' she said. 'In the early days, there were negative, dark places. I think that's inevitable. We don't now have negative thoughts; we're actually a lot stronger, a lot more hopeful. We have to be hopeful, it's what keeps us going, keeps us focused. It was such a relaxing holiday and, up until that night, it was as good a holiday as we've had with the children, up until that point.'

They were asked, point blank, if they thought Madeleine was still alive. 'Absolutely,' said Kate. She motioned to Madeleine's favourite toy, which she now carried around. 'It's something that Madeleine has with her every night,' she said. 'If she's upset or not well, she has Cuddle Cat. It's provided me with a little bit of comfort, something of Madeleine close to me... The first forty-eight to seventy-two hours were, as you can imagine, quite dark and difficult to function. Since that time, through people's help, we have got a lot stronger. We're very lucky that we've got a fantastic family, really good friends. Even people who don't know us at all have been amazing. The support we've had has been overwhelming and it's that that's kept us strong and hopeful that we will see Madeleine back with us. It's true to say that the first two days we didn't eat much or sleep much but since then things have picked up and we have been able to be stronger.'

Gerry also spoke of those first, awful days. 'At the end of that first week, we had spent so much emotion,' he said. 'We actually had a period when we felt completely devoid of emotion. The analogy I like to use is it's like when you

Madeleine at home in Rothley, Leicestershire, wearing the jersey of her favourite football team, Everton.

The Ocean Club resort in Praia da Luz, Portugal, where Madeleine went missing on 3 May 2007.

The Ocean Club resort and the surrounding area.

The last photograph of Madeleine. It was taken by Kate on the afternoon that Madeleine went missing.

Kate and Gerry McCann on their way to release balloons marking the fiftieth day of Madeleine's disappearance.

Gerry and Kate meet the Pope – who blesses a picture of Maddy – as part of a series of trips to raise awareness of Madeleine's disappearance.

Premiership stars, such as Robbie Keane (above), show their support for the find Madeleine campaign.

The man with the glass eye: Robert Murat was the first official suspect in Madeleine's disappearance.

Police officers cordon off the area surrounding Casa Liliana, the house of Robert Murat.

were students, and you've got your overdraft limit and you've gone beyond it and there's nothing left in the tank. Physically and mentally we were shattered but it's gradually got back on more of an even keel. We're back into the black. And we've also worked tirelessly behind the scenes to put support mechanisms in place, including our legal team.'

As for the reaction across the world, he was very grateful for all the support they received. 'It's touched everyone,' he said. 'You don't have to be a parent for this to have a major impact on you. The worst feeling was helplessness. But once you start to do things you start to feel a bit better and I hope that we are going to look back at the end of all this and say that we have done everything in our power. We pray that something like this doesn't happen again, but when it does, the speed of the next response and the template that we've set will ultimately ...

'There's been so much goodwill and humanity out there, it really has restored ... One evil act actually has resulted in so much good. Those first few days were the darkest place and every parent's worst nightmare. That first Sunday, we went to church, every single person came up to me and said, "We'll get Madeleine back." That certainly galvanised me and I'm not the most religious person in the world, but I got tremendous strength out of that. The only thing that will truly make us feel good is Madeleine's return, there's no doubt about that.'

The church was helping them. The couple had been going to mass every day, praying for Madeleine's return, and this in turn touched the Pope so much that a meeting was arranged after talks between the Vatican and Roman Catholic Church in Britain. The McCanns were to fly to Rome to meet Benedict XVI on a private jet offered by the retail magnate Sir Philip Green, as Kate wanted to make the trip as short as possible. 'Kate does not want to be away from the twins for any length of time, and she does not want to leave Portugal,' said a source. 'She is determined to stay here as a base until Madeleine is found.'

Nonetheless, the meeting clearly meant a great deal to the couple. 'The McCanns have found their faith a great source of comfort,' said a source in Portugal. 'They are pleased that the Pope has agreed to provide further spiritual guidance. They will be introduced to the Holy Father, who has been kept informed of the progress of their campaign to find Madeleine. It's highly unusual to be granted an audience of that nature. It also serves another purpose, of keeping the campaign in the consciousness of Europeans.'

Clarence Mitchell, Foreign Office liaison officer, gave more information. 'I can confirm that approaches have been made to Cardinal Cormac Murphy O'Connor and to the British ambassador to the Holy See,' he said. 'We are certainly exploring the possibility of Gerry and Kate McCann visiting Rome to meet the Pope in the near future.'

Other visits were also planned: to Madrid, Seville, Berlin and Amsterdam. They were hoping to meet David Beckham in Madrid: it all kept the family in the public eye.

Unsurprisingly, the couple were finding it hard to let the twins out of their sight. 'The twins sleep in bed with us now,' said Kate. 'We have become totally protective parents. They help us get through this. They were so close to Madeleine, only twenty months apart.' She also revealed quite how long the couple had had to wait for Maddy's arrival. 'We married in 1998 and Madeleine was born in 2003,' she said. 'We had to wait five years. Finding out I was pregnant was unbelievable. We had tried for so long. She was everything to us.'

And of course, there was the delicate matter of how to behave towards the twins who, young as they were, must have noticed that their sister had disappeared. 'The twins are so young and they just get on with things, but obviously we don't want them to forget about Madeleine,' said Kate. 'We are hoping to see a child psychologist next week to explain to the twins what has happened to Madeleine. My waking thought is that the phone by the bedside has not rung and that means Madeleine has not been found. I am better in the morning; it seems like a fresh start. Evenings are harder. I haven't been able to use the camera since I took that last photo of her.'

But there continued to be concerns about how long the police had taken to react. The McCanns were still being very careful not to criticise the police, but they couldn't hold back the odd comment. 'A lot of people have come forward this week,' said Kate. 'We've been surprised how long it's taken. I hope she is still in Portugal because if that's the case, the scope of this investigation means it should be just a matter of time before they find her, but the borders were not closed until ten the next morning.'

Back in Portugal, the police had enlisted the help of mobile phone experts, of the type that helped convict the Soham murderer Ian Huntley. They were to focus on calls made by Robert Murat, to find out exactly where he was the night Maddy went missing, something similar specialists had done to prove that Huntley was not where he said he was. 'These specialists were crucial in Soham and could be equally valuable in Portugal,' a police chief said. 'Murat remains the only suspect and his records will be scrutinised in great detail. If there are any inconsistencies between his records and his statement, he will be questioned again.'

Meanwhile, Kate and Gerry released some video footage showing Madeleine larking around as the family set off on holiday – it was the last video that was taken of her. She was seen eagerly climbing up the steps of the plane to fly to the Algarve. In another clip she was seen clasping her Barbie rucksack, which was displayed as the film was released, slipping and grazing her shin on the plane steps. Madeleine started to cry, but her excitement was such she stopped almost immediately. 'She was really brave,' said Gerry, who was holding the pink rucksack. 'She started crying, but stopped almost immediately. It would usually have caused ten minutes of crying rather than ten seconds.' It was almost unbelievable what had happened since.

The Search Continues

The visit to the Vatican went ahead as planned: a visibly moved Kate and Gerry McCann met the Pope, who laid his hands on a photograph of Madeleine and prayed for the safe return of the little girl. Meanwhile, back in Portugal, the police came under renewed attack for not searching empty apartments close to where Madeleine had disappeared. Many had metal shutters to keep the sun out, which in turn would have made it impossible to see if anyone was inside.

Michael Askew, 60, a British businessman who owns a two-bedroom apartment close to the complex, was astonished by what he saw as the ineptitude of the police. 'I'm amazed the police haven't searched my place,' said Mr Askew, who owns a building company in Derbyshire. 'Soon after Madeleine was abducted, I saw an interview on television with a Portuguese policeman who said they had master keys to all the nearby properties. He said they were going to be searched, but mine certainly hasn't. My son Robert went out there this week for the first time since Madeleine went missing and it's obvious no one's been into the apartment.

He's spoken to the neighbours and they say none of theirs have been searched, either. I've spoken to the complex managers and they say they haven't handed in the master keys to anyone. I'm also surprised that no one seems to have been asked whether they were staying in the apartments or who may have been renting them at the time. That would seem a very obvious thing to have done. It makes you very sceptical about how they have run their investigation.'

It did indeed, and further evidence of ineptitude emerged when it became clear that a description of a man seen carrying a child on the night Maddy disappeared was wrong: the police had given his height as being three inches taller than the witness had said. It appears there had been a mistake in the conversion from centimetres to inches.

Refusing to let themselves be bowed down by events, the McCanns flew to Madrid as part of their ongoing campaign to keep Maddy's disappearance in the news. Of course, this meant leaving the twins behind, something they clearly found extremely difficult. 'Leaving them is really hard,' said Kate. 'From a selfish point of view, we would have liked to have had them with us for comfort, but it is not best for them.' Indeed, they were still being shielded from what had happened and had no idea Maddy was gone. The sympathy of the world, meanwhile, was as strong as ever: the Find Madeleine fund now stood at £374,000.

A note of desperation seemed to enter the proceedings when it emerged that the police were turning to psychics for help. The Portuguese police had compiled two dossiers full of messages from clairvoyants and, indeed, psychics had been used in many investigations beforehand, from the hunt for the Yorkshire Ripper to the disappearance of the teenager Milly Dowler. Several said that Maddy had been taken over the border into Spain. Even so, it did rather suggest that the police didn't have a great deal more to go on: 'If there are indications there is enough to follow, we will go,' said Chief Inspector Olegario Sousa, when asked about the danger of hoaxers. 'If there aren't, we can not do anything.'

While in Madrid, the McCanns spoke again of their plight and the hope that Maddy was taken by someone who would look after her. 'We pray she is being looked after and that it's someone who wanted a little girl of their own and would look after her well,' he said. 'But we don't know who has taken her and it doesn't help in the search. We hope that whoever has got her will give her up voluntarily. We haven't ruled out that whoever has got her drops her off in a church or a safe place. We have considered all scenarios, as everyone has. We have no evidence to suggest that there has been any harm done to Madeleine. We pray she is alive and well and we dwell on the positive.'

The McCanns had also been told that there was a possible

link to the disappearance of a seven-year-old Spanish boy called Yeremi Vargas, who had vanished from his home on Gran Canaria the previous March. 'I know the Portuguese and Spanish police work closely in other criminal investigations,' said Gerry. 'I would like some reassurance in Spain there has been some proactive investigation. It's at least worth exploring the possibility Madeleine's disappearance should be put in the context of other disappearances in the Iberian peninsula.'

Early in June, nearly a month after Madeleine had gone missing, there was what seemed to be a major breakthrough. There appeared to be DNA evidence of an intruder into the room Madeleine had been sleeping in, which not only didn't match any of the McCann family, but also didn't match Robert Murat or Sergey Malinka. 'There is a new suspect,' said a Portuguese police source. 'This could be vital evidence in the search for Madeleine. Tests detected DNA corresponding to six people in the bedroom. Five were linked to the McCann family, the other shows there was a stranger in Madeleine's bedroom.'

Unfortunately, it did not tell who that stranger was. Portugal doesn't have a DNA database, and so the sample was passed on to British police in the hope that they might be able to match it. Officials couldn't help but sound a note of caution. 'It is an important step in the investigation, but the truth is that the DNA cannot be matched with any records,' said a source at the Instituto Nacional de Medecina Legal Laboratory in Coimbra. 'The evidence is very vague.' Robert Murat, at least, was pleased. Tuck Price said his client 'welcomed' the new evidence, and hoped it would help clear his name. He was warned, though, that he still might face charges relating to the pornography found on his computer.

The McCanns continued their tour across Europe, visiting the Netherlands, Morocco and Germany before flying back to Spain.

Back in Britain, the family was doing all it could to keep Madeleine in the news. Diane and John McCann joined children from the Bankhead Primary School in Rutherglen, Glasgow, to release four hundred yellow balloons with pictures of Maddy attached. Diane was a teacher at the school. 'It was a beautiful sight,' she said. 'The family is delighted with the efforts of the pupils and my colleagues. Who knows how far the balloons will fly?' A similar display also took place in Northern Ireland, when primary school children released balloons with messages of hope attached. Meanwhile, to date, one thousand pictures had been uploaded to the website.

There was also talk about establishing a special Madeleine Day, to be marked by a global pop concert with the likes of Sir Elton John publicising the case. Sir Elton had been playing a DVD of Madeleine at recent concerts and it was thought that a host of big names stars could appear from around the world. 'One of the ideas is maybe getting all of the people who have publicly supported us to come together,' said Gerry. 'I don't just mean from the UK, but from different parts of the world. We want a big event to raise awareness that she is still missing. We would look at high profile people who have already pledged support. It will be some sort of focus around an anniversary, to tell people Madeleine's still missing. I think it would be later this year, once media attention has dropped, to bring it back up, hopefully, for a short period. It wouldn't be a one-year anniversary; it would be sooner than that.

'What we're doing at the minute has its role, but doing that down the line in a few months won't have anything like the same impact. We might have a sporting event, something arts, something music. We've had backing from sporting people up to now. We have had backing from certain musical celebrities as well. We've got some other musical contacts that we were exploring, who are happy to offer support. We're not saying it would necessarily be one big concert; it might be that on a certain day they are playing her DVD. What we want at the current time is maximum message out there now about her disappearance, but then just events to bring it back up occasionally to remind people if she's not found.'

It was a measure of how professional the campaign to keep Madeleine in the spotlight had become. There was a short-term strategy, as well as a longer-term strategy – and also, perhaps for the first time on the part of the parents, an acceptance that Madeleine might never be found. Difficult as it must have been to discuss, Gerry acknowledged what was on so many minds. 'Of course we believe Madeleine is still alive, but you would be incredible if you hadn't considered the worst scenario, that she's dead,' he said. 'Kate and I discuss it – not a lot, but we talk about hope and that while there's some, we will not give up. At the minute, there's loads of hope.'

Kate herself was still clinging to Maddy's Cuddle Cat. 'We don't know where she is,' she said. 'We'd like to think she might still be in Portugal. But we know there's a possibility she's gone over a border – or several borders. We know there are bad people out there, but we also know there are a lot of sad people. We hope it's the latter.'

Worldwide support remained as strong as ever: at the Epsom Derby, all the jockeys wore yellow ribbons to highlight the fact that Madeleine was still missing. The initiative was thought up by Martin Dwyer, who rode Regime, and who himself has two children. 'People all over the globe are watching the Derby, and we owe it to this little girl to do what we can to help,' he said.

There was a new theory about Madeleine's disappearance: that she had been abducted for a ransom demand and then the kidnapper had got cold feet. 'Many motives have been suggested, including kidnap for a ransom,' said Chief Inspector Olegario Sousa. 'Whoever took the child could have had the objective of ransom but not demanded it because they panicked after all the attention the case has received. Who would ask for money for the girl, when her image is running round the world? A kidnapper could have the child well hidden, close by. After thirty days, there is nothing to state that the girl is dead.'

Unsurprisingly, the McCanns declared themselves willing to sell their £600,000 house in Rothley to get her back. 'If we thought we had the money under our control, and thought it would secure her safe return, we would sell our house, we would do anything to get our daughter back,' Gerry said. 'We wouldn't rule out that financial inducement might help us find her, through one route or another.'

The two were continuing their tour around Europe to highlight Maddy's disappearance when a shockwave was sent around the world. It occurred at a news conference in Berlin when, for the first time ever, it was publicly suggested that the McCanns might have been involved in some way in their daughter's disappearance. Of course, since then, those theories have grown to such an extent that Gerry and Kate have been named as suspects by the Portuguese police, but both then and now anyone who read anything about the case would be hard pressed to say they were involved: it would have taken acting on a scale most professional thespians couldn't manage, let alone a grief-stricken, middle-class family caught up in a global spotlight they never would have sought. It would have involved a cover-up beyond the realms of possibility: it simply did not ring true. And yet this suspicion had, perhaps inevitably, been raised in some quarters, for the simple reason that with the possible exception of Robert Murat – and the case against him was going nowhere – there was nobody else to blame.

Even so, there was a sense of shock when Sabina Mueller, a German radio reporter, faced the couple and asked, 'How do you feel about the fact that more and more people appear to be pointing the finger at you, saying the way you behave is not the way people normally behave when their child is abducted? They seem to imply you might have had something to do with it.'

Up until that moment, Kate had left Gerry to do most of the talking, but she clearly couldn't let this one pass. Looking quite appalled, she grabbed the microphone and said, 'To be honest, I don't actually think that is the case.

I think there is a very small minority of people that are criticising us. The facts are, we were dining very close to the children and we were checking up on them very, very regularly. You know, we are very responsible parents and we love our children so much. I think it is very few people that are actually criticising us.'

Gerry was equally upset. 'I have never heard before that anyone considers us suspects in this,' he said, his voice audibly shaking. 'The Portuguese police certainly don't. Without going in to too much detail about the circumstances, we were with a large group of people. There is absolutely no way Kate and I are involved in this abduction. I can understand why people are amazed at what Kate and I are doing. Before this happened to us we would have been amazed. I'm sure everyone in this room has asked, "How can you continue to function when your daughter, who you love so much, has been taken?" In the first two or three days we were almost non-functional. One of the worst feelings, along with the terror and the anguish and the despair, was the helplessness.

'We hope and pray every single day that this finishes and Madeleine is returned to us safely. We don't want a long campaign. We just want her back. We have got to keep going, we believe she is alive. There is an absence of evidence to the contrary. We think it is more likely that she is alive than not alive. Everything we have done has been by taking counsel from experts. We have taken strength, not just from the people who have supported us, but also by being active in the search. If we had stayed indoors, locked ourselves away and just waited and waited for a month, we would be the shells of people we are.'

Indeed, there was a palpable sense that a line had been crossed with the question. It was not only Gerry and Kate who were distressed, but millions of others, people who had never met the family, but had come to care about the case, too. It was (and remains) inconceivable that the McCanns had anything to do with it. It simply added to the burden they had to bear.

Indeed, a source close to the family expressed their disgust. 'Gerry and Kate were quite surprised at the question, but they answered it firmly, to the point, and dismissed it out of hand,' they said. 'It is a complete travesty to suggest something like that. It implies all sorts of things and is totally and utterly untrue. Quite frankly, I am surprised they didn't walk out there and then. But in keeping with the people they are, they maintained their dignity and moved on.'

The press conference had been held at the Berlin Press Centre, and was one of many taking place in the trip across Europe. It was that trip and the McCanns unwavering dignity in the face of torment that made some people believe they were too cold and too calm. It was almost as if some people wanted hysteria or breakdown, not two devastated parents, who nonetheless kept matters going for the sake of the rest of their family.

'Our primary objective today is to appeal to German tourists, and to reach the maximum number of people we have done a series of short television interviews and paper interviews,' said Gerry, explaining why they were taking the actions they were. 'This is not a European tour. We are coming to centres that we think can influence the search and we are coming with very specific goals. We always ask ourselves before we do anything publicly, "What is our objective and how will it help?". What we cannot do is look back in six months' time and say, I wish we had done this and I wish we had done that. These are very short intense periods of media activity. The only successful outcome for us is to get Madeleine back. I do not fully understand the reasons it has generated so much publicity.'

Kate was also keen to emphasise that they were not taking extended periods away from home. 'It is not easy,' she said. 'It is important to point out that a day like today is very intense, but it is just a day. We do have a lot of time back with the children, with Sean and Amelie.'

Indeed, the children were both a solace and yet something else to worry about. 'We are lucky we have Amelie and Sean,' said Gerry. 'We love them very much. They are toddlers – they don't understand what's happening. They need love and attention. It is very difficult for us to leave them, but we are leaving them with Madeleine's godparents and Kate's parents. They will look after them and are happy. We try to stay away for as little time as possible. I have to say that when we have family time just on our own, it is very difficult because Madeleine's not there.'

While in Germany, the McCanns met the Deputy Justice Minister Lutz Diwell. The conversation, obviously, centred on Madeleine, but it also broadened to the arc of child abduction generally, and how Maddy's case could be used to publicise the problem as far as other children were concerned. 'We realise the publicity Madeleine's case is getting is raising the issue of child abuse in general,' he said. 'Governments and particularly the EU have to address this issue. It is as good a time as ever to start a debate about this kind of thing.'

Indeed, the McCanns had even considered going to Strasbourg to raise support from MEPs. 'I think this is the first foreign national abduction of its kind since 1991. It's extremely rare,' he said. 'What we are doing is being associated with child abuse in its broadest terms, sex offenders and trafficking of people. We're not upset that Madeleine's abduction is being associated with these wider issues.'

Meanwhile, the McCanns were launching a wristband to keep high the awareness of Madeleine's case.

The furore surrounding Sabine Mueller's question, however, did not go away. Many people continued to be shocked that she'd asked it in the first place, and she defended her actions the following day. 'I was aware it was a difficult question, but I felt it was a question that needed to be asked,' she said. 'I do not suspect the McCanns of being involved. I know it has been seen as a hard question, but I did not think it was improper. I did not want to hurt these people. I thought that when he replied, Gerry McCann was very calm. Either they are very good actors or they are telling the truth. If they had walked out I would have been sorry.

'They are putting themselves out there a lot. If they keep staging press conferences, they have to expect uncomfortable questions. I was doing my job as a journalist and don't want to be drawn into anything more. There was an interview this morning on the radio with a criminal psychologist who was saying that in up to ninety-five per cent of cases where children disappear or are killed, it is by somebody in their immediate circle. I said to my boyfriend that this wasn't the case, because they were away from home and on holiday. He [the expert] wasn't talking about this case specifically. He was talking generally. I was having a private discussion with my boyfriend that led me to ask this question. I framed the question so I wasn't making an allegation. I asked about the people who were being critical and had started pointing the finger.'

Yet another red herring was thrown up while the McCanns were still in Berlin, actually en route to Tempelhof airport on their way to Amsterdam. They delayed their flight as soon as they heard the news. Investigative journalist Antonio Toscano, a Spaniard who covered missing persons stories, reported that a Spanish paedophile had been hired by two other people to kidnap Madeleine. The man had been spotted in a bar in Seville, which was just two hours away from the Spanish border, about a week before Maddy's disappearance, and fitted the description of a man seen carrying away a child in his arms. 'The man had already been imprisoned for a paedophile case outside Spain,' said a source. 'He was hired by two other people to abduct Madeleine, who had been identified some time before she disappeared, possibly in the UK.'

There were also reports that the Spanish police had taken a 'credible call' from a man who said that he knew where Maddy was being held, and wanted to talk personally to her parents. 'A man called saying he knew where Madeleine was and wanted to speak to the McCanns,' said a source within the Spanish police. 'This did not appear to be a crank call and the information was felt credible enough to warrant the couple being informed immediately. After three hours, the urgency of the situation waned, but it remains an important new lead and inquiries continue. The McCanns have always said it might only take one phone call to get Madeleine back. They are still waiting for that call.' As the McCanns were told he might try to make contact, they delayed their flight: as so often before, it all came to nil. They went on to Amsterdam, where they had lived for a year with Maddy when Kate was pregnant with the twins.

It was not long before eyebrows were raised yet again by the behaviour of the Portuguese police. This time round, the problem was a culture clash as much as anything else, for the problem appeared to be drinking at lunch. At the very same time the McCanns were facing that rather brutal press conference in Berlin, Chief Inspector Olegario Sousa and one of his detectives, Goncalo Amaral, were pictured enjoying a two-hour lunch, complete with wine and whisky. Chief Inspector Sousa was defensive. 'It is very, very sad, but a person's free time is for lunch,' he said. 'That is a normal thing to do.'

Worse still, the men were heard discussing the case in front of other diners. 'If it were detectives from Scotland Yard, there would be an absolute uproar,' said Philomena McCann. 'But we have to let them get on with their work, because that's all we have to rely on. We have to accept their approach because the British government will not intervene and take over. It is a different culture where they have lunches and siestas but we hope the work is made up at other times.'

Matters worsened shortly afterwards. Philomena and a cousin went to Lisbon airport to put up 'missing' posters for Maddy (incredibly, none had been hung there, allegedly because the Portuguese government will not allow any such posters, for fear of damaging the tourist trade), and were promptly expelled from the airport by gun-toting police. 'They just don't want to admit a child was snatched in their country,' she said angrily, revealing that Kate had asked her to put the posters up.

'Kate was really distraught when she got to the airport and there were no posters of Madeleine,' she said. 'I couldn't believe what happened when we got there. I was given permission to put the posters up by a woman on the information desk. But straight away we were swooped on by two armed police officers. We thought it was a misunderstanding and tried to explain, but they wouldn't listen. My relative was bodily manhandled by them. I contacted the director of the airport, Dr Francisco Severino. He said we couldn't put the posters up but said that if we went away and sent him a fax, he would consider it. We lost a valuable opportunity to get our message to thousands of air travellers who come through the terminal. It seemed clear they didn't want negativity affecting tourism. Surely if people think the police and the authorities are doing everything they can to find Madeleine, other families visiting Portugal would feel more secure.'

Matters now seemed to be going from bad to worse. Goncalo Amaral, one of the most senior detectives in the hunt for Maddy, was revealed to be one of five officers formally accused of torturing a confession from Leonor Cipriano. She allegedly was attacked in September 2004 after her nine-year-old daughter Joana had gone missing from the village of Figueira, just seven miles from Praia da Luz.

The parallels with Madeleine's case were eerie. The police hadn't sealed off the house, allowing hundreds of police and friends of the family to walk all over the crime scene and ended up accusing Joana's mother of the crime. The body was never found, but Leonor and her brother Joao were eventually convicted of killing her: however, she later claimed that the police had beaten a confession out of her, while pictures showed her face and body covered in bruises. She lodged a complaint about what had happened, which was taken up by the public prosecutor's office, while a police trades union official said the injuries occurred when she fell down stairs.

Five policemen were said to be involved: three accused of torture, a fourth for failing to stop the attack and a fifth for falsifying paperwork. Amaral was one of the five: even so, he remained on the case searching for Maddy.

Meanwhile, it became clear that the mystery caller who said he had news of Maddy's whereabouts had nothing of the sort: he had merely been trying to extort £500,000 from the Find Madeleine fund.

The McCanns put on a very brave face and journeyed to Morocco, where quite a few people believed Madeleine was. There was a huge trade in stolen children in Morocco: they were taught how to beg on the streets and, in Marrakech, could earn up to three hundred euros a day.

And the couple had other worries, too. There were reports that Gerry and Kate were at odds over what to do next: he wanted to return home to continue the search from England, where he believed he could do more, while Kate could not bear the thought of leaving Portugal without her missing child. In the light of this, again, it is hard to see how anyone could really believe the McCanns were involved in the disappearance of their daughter – but even so, matters were going to get worse for them in the months ahead.

Antonio Toscano was still on the scene, still asserting that he knew who had taken Madeleine, but his presence was not proving helpful for the McCanns. 'As soon as Mr Toscano contacted us via an intermediary, we immediately spoke to him,' said Clarence Mitchell, the former BBC reporter who had become the official spokesman for the McCanns. 'At every stage Mr Toscano declined to provide a name for the suspect he believed was responsible for Madeleine's abduction. This was both frustrating and potentially hurtful to Gerry and Kate. They were upset that this man appeared to be trying to give us important information but when asked the critical questions declined to do so.'

Toscano himself told a very different story, insisting he knew the full name of the person responsible, someone he described as 'The Frenchman'. He had received a tip-off, he said, before bumping in to the Frenchman at a bar in Seville. 'I am one hundred per cent certain this is the man who kidnapped Madeleine McCann,' he said. 'I have spoken to the police in Spain and Portugal but they have still not checked out the information. The Portuguese police said they did not want me to tell them the name over the phone but they have not sent anyone to interview me.

'All I want to do is to meet the police and tell them what I know. I am prepared to do this immediately. I am fully aware that if I was not one hundred per cent right the information I have revealed would be very upsetting to Madeleine's family, but I am certain I am. I believe she is alive and probably being held in Portugal. The sooner this is investigated the better the chance of a good conclusion to this sad story. I just want the little girl to be returned safely to her family.'

So did everyone else. The frustration was palpable: Maddy had been missing for six weeks now, and despite countless leads, theories and chasings after red herrings, no one had any clearer an idea about what had happened to her than on the night that she first disappeared.

A Cruel Hoax

A couple of weeks into June, and matters became really ugly. The Portuguese police received an anonymous letter purporting to know the location of Madeleine's body – a letter that was taken seriously as the police believed it came from a man who had successfully identified the grave of two girls murdered by paedophiles in Belgium the previous year. The letter had been sent to the Dutch newspaper *De Telegraaf* in Amsterdam, which in turn passed it on to the Portuguese police: it said that Madeleine was buried in deserted scrubland, near the town of Odiaxere, east of Praia da Luz, 'north of the road under branches and rocks, around six to seven metres off the road.' A detailed map accompanied it.

Unsurprisingly, Kate and Gerry, who had been read the letter by a Portuguese policeman before he realised what he was translating, were devastated by the news. Kate was in tears: 'They found the whole thing very upsetting,' said a family friend. 'They are both on tenterhooks waiting for further news. It is being taken as seriously as any other line of inquiry.'

The Dutch police certainly thought there was something in it. 'With the tip about the Belgian disappearance in the back of our minds, this letter grabbed our attention,' said Dutch police spokesman Rob Van der Veen. 'The writer of that letter had closely pinpointed the area where the girls' bodies were eventually found. That particular letter was posted in Rotterdam the day before the bodies were found. We are therefore not ruling out the fact that this letter regarding Madeleine could be very important. While this letter is slightly less professional than the one regarding the Belgian children, we are looking at it seriously and we are in contact with the Portuguese police.'

The case involving the Belgian children had some horrible similarities to Maddy's, at least as far as the disappearance was concerned. Two step sisters, Nathalie Mahy, ten, and Stacey Lemmens, seven, had been playing in the street outside a bar in the town of Liege, while their parents were having dinner nearby. They vanished and were later found to have been murdered by a paedophile ring: their bodies were found in a sewer just half a mile from the location the letter writer had pointed to. It was a horribly unsettling development.

The contents of the letter had been made public, which Gerry called 'insensitive and cruel.' He continued, 'One can imagine how upsetting it is for Kate and I to hear of such claims through the media.' And indeed, locals and ex-pats had already started to search the scene with dogs – while the police themselves had yet to start a search.

Eventually, the police did conduct a very comprehensive search of the scrubland and, as much as anything in this unhappy saga could be said to have a happy ending, this one did. No body was found. The McCanns, of course, had been put through yet more suffering and the police admitted as much: 'We think it is a cruel hoax,' said a police source. 'We have found no sign of any kind of evidence. It seems more and more likely that it is made up.' Police chief Olegario Sousa, the subject of so much criticism, seemed a little weary. 'This clue has been completely checked and the result was checked, so the investigation goes on,' he said.

The McCanns were relieved enormously. Gerry had been running a blog on the Find Madeleine website and now wrote, 'I'm glad to say that following yesterday's letter in the *Telegraaf*, there has been no evidence that Madeleine is in the area indicated. It is six weeks since Madeleine disappeared. We believe that Madeleine is alive.'

Kate revealed that a psychologist had been helping the family to cope. 'We couldn't get out of our heads that she was likely to be dead and we were truly, truly grieving,' she said. 'But then the psychologist said, "Is there any other possibility?" And then he started channelling negatives and saying,

"Of course there are other possibilities." And we started to see that.'

Those were very brave words from a couple that had been forced to confront the worst, but there was no gainsaying the fact that the investigation was a mess. Chief Inspector Sousa actually decided to blame the family for allowing so many people into their apartment in the immediate aftermath of Maddy's disappearance, as if the family wasn't desperate to enlist as much help as possible: 'The presence of so many people in the room where the little girl slept with her brother and sister could have complicated the work of the forensic team,' he said. 'At worst, they would have destroyed all the evidence. This could prove fatal for the investigation.'

It looked very much as if he was trying to shift the blame for the incompetence of the investigation away from the police force, and while the McCanns themselves didn't say anything, sources close to the family voiced their dismay. 'It's insensitive,' said a family friend. 'Of course the family are going to search the apartment. If your child goes missing, you search under beds, in wardrobes, everywhere.'

Increasingly, it seemed as though the McCanns were doing the police's job. Attending a church service in Praia da Luz – Kate was still clutching Cuddle Cat – Gerry recalled that it was Father's Day back in England. He had already had to endure both his and Maddy's birthdays without his eldest child, and he could hardly bear to think about the same day the previous year. 'I can't think about how we spent it,' he said. 'I can't think about anything except how to get Madeleine back.'

Indeed, the family was campaigning as actively as ever to highlight what had happened, and this had now broadened into a campaign to highlight the plight of other missing children as well. To mark the fifty days since Maddy's disappearance, plans were made to release fifty balloons in fifty different countries, including Germany, France, Australia, Dubai, Canada, America and El Salvador. 'We will probably have ten centres in the UK, such as Glasgow, Liverpool, Leicester, as well as Ireland and Guernsey, where we have friends,' Gerry said. 'We are going to tie it in with other missing kids. We were anxious about going to their countries and asking for help in finding Madeleine. But they have said to us, "What you are doing is amazing and it is helping us."'

Back in Portugal, the police investigation seemed to have stalled. There was widespread criticism when the police again searched the apartment from which Maddy had gone missing – a full seven weeks after her disappearance. Why, observers asked, was there any doubt that the crime scene had not already been properly searched? 'It is astonishing that they are still at the stage of scouring the crime scene for clues,' said one. 'You would think that everything that could have yielded information had already been gathered up. It's a pretty damning sign that the investigation is going nowhere.'

It was indeed. Gerry returned to England, for only the second time since Madeleine disappeared, in order to appoint a campaign chief for what was now called the 'Leaving No Stone Unturned' appeal. It now stood at £720,000. His compassionate leave of absence from Leicester's Glenfield Hospital was due to expire at the end of June, only a week and a half away, but as he was telling colleagues, he was not in a good state of mind to return to work as a doctor.

The situation was agonising for everyone concerned, but Gerry was able to put his medical skills to some good use: an elderly passenger collapsed on the flight from Faro to Gatwick, and Gerry was able to help. 'The crew were full of praise for Gerry and grateful for his expert help,' said a spokesman for easyJet.

But it was a rare moment of normality in an increasingly difficult situation. And as if this were all not bad enough, a pickpocket stole Gerry's wallet during his visit to London: he bent over to pick up his shoulder bag, and as he did so, a thief snatched the wallet. It contained two unpublished pictures of Maddy, a detail that seemed, somehow, to make the family's situation even worse. Philomena McCann was beside herself. 'How can you do that to someone who's been through what he has?' she demanded. 'He's already demoralised enough and to be put on the back foot like this – you can't believe people would stoop so low. It was some dirty animal. We don't care about the money, but we do care about getting the pictures of Madeleine back that Gerry kept in the wallet. They were his favourites, really treasured pictures. They are irreplaceable.' She urged the thief to give back the pictures.

Susan Healy, Madeleine's grandmother, felt just the same, describing it as, 'yet another kick in the teeth. Gerry didn't see the thief take it, but it contained precious photographs which have now been lost forever,' she continued. 'There can't be many people who don't recognise Kate and Gerry now – shame on the thieves for doing it. Hopefully when they see the photos of Madeleine in the wallet, they will realise what they've done. I spoke to Kate last night, after she had spoken to Gerry. It sounded like she has had a rough few days, but was feeling a little better.'

It was at this time that Antonio Toscano decided to e-mail a picture and name of the man he accused of abducting Maddy to the police. 'I e-mailed the name and picture of the Frenchman to the Portuguese and Spanish police first thing Tuesday,' he said. 'I've also sent them names and pictures of the Frenchman's associates. They are men who have served sentences for paedophile crimes and are now back in the community.' But still it led nowhere.

The hunt switched abruptly to Malta. There had been five sightings of a girl thought to be Maddy, and the witnesses were so positive it was her whom they had seen that the, made a sworn statement before a judge. This led magistrate Miriam Hayman to start up an official investigation: the first sighting had been in the island's capital Valetta several days earlier. A little blonde girl had been seen with a man and a woman: an intensive search was launched immediately, but to no avail. Other sightings on the island had her with a woman, a man and an Arabic-looking couple.

Police throughout the country were given her photograph, while security was tightened up around the airport and various harbours. 'Police immediately initiated an investigation,' a spokesman for the Maltese police force confirmed. 'The individuals in question also gave evidence in front of an investigating magistrate. Due to ongoing investigations, it is unethical to furnish further information at this stage.' Interpol was alerted, while officers conducted searches around St George's Bay, an area popular with British tourists, and the Rivera Martinique Hotel. The head of Malta's vice squad, Assistant Commissioner Michael

Cassar was appointed to lead the case: he confirmed that the sightings were being considered to be significant.

'Officers are keeping a close eye on departures from the airport and various harbours,' said a source close to the case. 'There is also tightened security at Malta International Airport and other entry and exit points. Posters of Madeleine have gone up all over the island, and photographs have been distributed to police and officials working at the ports. According to yesterday's reports, the young girl was sighted during the last few days and she was not alone. According to my sources she was in the company of an adult. For security reasons no information was given as regards the location of the searches being carried out by the police. But according to my information, officers are focusing on areas familiar with tourists, mainly in the northern part of the island.'

As events progressed, the police issued detailed descriptions of a middle-aged white woman and a dark-skinned man in his late thirties who were allegedly both seen with the child. Less helpfully, an anonymous caller was also claiming to have seen Maddy, and it was thought he was calling from the village of Bahar-ic-Caghaq. It housed a rather seedy caravan site, alongside a large aquatic fun park. A local resident, Paul Gauci, explained what was going on.

'My wife and I have lived here a few years and we have never seen so many police cars,' he said. 'Morning, noon and night they have been driving past the camp and the pleasure park. We did think they were looking for something. There are no posters or pictures of the missing girl here, but we all recognise her face from the TV news.'

Mindful, perhaps, of the criticisms of the Portuguese police, Superintendent Mario Spiteri made it clear that the search was being taken extremely seriously. 'We have stepped up security in the area and I can assure you we're taking these reports very seriously indeed,' he said. 'The last time Madeleine was reported was in Bahar-ic-Caghac on 21 June by a man who would not reveal his name. We could not trace the call as it may have been made from a phone box. We are carrying out a search of the area and will continue our investigation until we can confidently rule out the claim. We are keeping our colleagues in the Portuguese police and Interpol up to date with our inquiry and I believe the information is being given to the little girl's family. I cannot say too much more at this time. There is a full-scale police investigation under way as well as an independent magisterial inquiry into these claims. If she is here on the island, it will be very hard for her captors to leave without us knowing. We have very little crime here and we are a very religious community.'

However, a note of caution was sounded from another source within the police force. 'I have my doubts about all these sightings,' he said. 'Once they became public, lots of people came forward claiming to have seen her. It's like a snowball effect. It's very unlikely that anyone would have brought her here, took her to the capital city, went on buses and walked around publicly when the world is searching for her. In any case, we're treating this case seriously. We never do a half-baked investigation. We're investigating at full blast.'

The McCanns said nothing. They were getting used to sightings that ended up coming to nothing – and indeed, that is what ultimately happened here. The Maltese police concluded that it was very unlikely she had ever been on the island at all.

The day came for the release of the fifty balloons in fifty different countries: three hundred similar events were held across the world to highlight the plight of missing children. Kate and Gerry were at the beach at Praia da Luz: it was 'overwhelming,' Gerry said. 'The global support gives us both strength and fresh determination to carry on our campaign,' he said.

The couple also chose that day to issue an open letter to the *Daily Express*, which had been doing a huge amount to keep Maddy's name and face in the spotlight. 'It is hard to express how much the support of your readers has helped us personally at this terribly difficult time,' they wrote. 'It has strengthened our resolve and supported our campaign enormously. We remain convinced that Madeleine is alive and will be returned to us safe and well with everyone's help.'

The heat now seemed to be very much off Robert Murat, but his family were becoming increasingly angry about the damage done to his name. Under Portuguese law he was not allowed to speak about the case personally, but he was happy for his relatives to do so, and they did. 'Robert is completely innocent, but his life has been ruined by the most disgusting and cruel allegations imaginable,' said his aunt, Sally Everleigh. 'His only crime was to want to do anything he could to help. As a father himself, he knew Kate and Gerry McCann must have been going through hell. He says he would happily take a lie detector test to prove his innocence. He has had hate mail – really awful stuff – and he thinks he will get physically attacked in the street. Robert has gone through some very dark moments and wondered if there was any point carrying on. At times he has been so low we have worried he is suicidal.'

Meanwhile, the McCann family had to deal with more practicalities. When such a terrible tragedy as theirs strikes, it seems that the mundane aspects of life should simply cease to exist, and yet they had to be tackled head on. They had to find somewhere new to live: they could still not countenance returning home without Maddy, but neither could they stay in the apartment they had been renting. 'If Madeleine is not found in the next couple of weeks, we need to move out of the apartment we're staying in as the family who own it are coming out for a holiday,' he said. 'I have to say, the owners have been extremely understanding, as they came to Praia da Luz for a holiday and relocated to another apartment to save us moving again. This degree of flexibility does not exist in the resort in the high season. We have managed to look at a few properties to rent in the next couple of days and I think we have found somewhere suitable to live until we return to the UK with Madeleine.'

There were also the couple's jobs to think about. A locum had been appointed to cover Kate's part time work as a GP, but Gerry's case was more difficult, and he needed to talk to his bosses about what he was going to do.

And there was palpable frustration that the investigation was quite clearly going nowhere. Yet again, it was the McCanns who were forced to take the initiative: 'We met with Portuguese and British police for an update,' Gerry said. 'Both Kate and myself raised the question of what someone should do if they think they see Madeleine. The clear advice is to call the local police as soon as possible, or someone working in an official capacity such as hotel staff or a tour representative. Please note that the emergency police numbers are variable in each country and for those going on holiday, it might be a good idea to enter the number on your mobile phone. If there is a car involved, please remember to record the registration number if possible.' It might be asked why Gerry, in the middle of all of his grief, was being forced to ask people to do all this, but there was no one else.

Towards the end of June, arrests finally were made in connection with the case, but they were not the arrests everyone was hoping for. Rather, the police took in an Italian, Danilo Chemello, and his Portuguese girlfriend, Aurora Pereira Vaz, after a dawn raid on the Costa del Sol town of Sotogrande, on suspicion of trying to extort reward money from the McCanns. It was thought that they had claimed to know where Madeleine was being held and wanted £2.5 million to relay the information onwards. It hadn't worked.

It tuned out that Chemello had a criminal record, and had spent some years in jail in France, though not for paedophile-related offences. 'He was sentenced to three years in France for mistreating his family,' said a police source in Rome. 'He is not suspected of kidnapping Madeleine, but a search of his home found material that warranted him being held in connection with her disappearance.'

The other parties involved treated the news rather warily. 'We have nothing to say, because we know no more than has been seen on the news,' said John McCann. 'We are treating these developments like all the others,' said Justine McGuiness, a spokesman for the McCanns. 'There is an ongoing investigation and the family is concentrating on that.'

Chief Inspector Olegario Sousa said that the Portuguese police force had been kept up to speed with events. 'We are keeping an open mind, but at the moment we believe these people were involved in trying to extort money from the McCann reward,' he said. 'We still don't know if there is a direct connection between these people and Madeleine, but Portuguese police were notified of the arrest because of a possible link.'

A little more information emerged about the couple who were not, to put it mildly, salubrious sorts. They had been jailed in 2004 for treating Vaz's five-year-old daughter like an animal, forcing her to eat dog food from a bowl on the floor. It turned out that Chemello was wanted in France for attempting to blackmail a judge; the police, meanwhile, described Vaz as being 'without scruples.'

A police statement was released: 'The National Police have arrested a couple, an Italian man and a Portuguese woman, in Sotogrande, Cadiz,' it read. 'Police started to investigate them to establish if they have tried to contact Madeleine's parents in order to claim the reward on offer.

The facts point to them both being fraudsters, although the police investigation is not closed. In the course of these investigations, officers discovered that the man had an outstanding arrest warrant issued by France over a crime of belonging to a criminal association. Furthermore, this person completed a sentence of eighteen months in prison in France for mistreating a minor. Police carried out the arrest on the basis of the order issued by France, and the attempt to claim the reward issued by Madeleine's parents.' Two young children who were living with the couple were taken into care by the local authority: it was a nasty episode, all round.

There was a small amount of comfort for the McCanns when the photographs that had been stolen with Gerry's wallet were returned. The wallet was sent back anonymously, minus the £100 in cash it had been carrying, but with the photographs, which meant a great deal more. It was a rare ray of sunshine in an increasingly sad tale. 'Our friends brought back my wallet, which had been returned, needless to say minus the sterling, although all my cards and thirty euros were still in it,' Gerry said. 'It's good to have my driving licence back, but the photographs are the most important things. I'm so glad to have got them back.'

Brian Kennedy, Madeleine's great-uncle, agreed. 'From what we can tell, it was posted about 8.15pm on the evening it was stolen,' he said. 'Either someone with a conscience realised who they had stolen it from and decided to return it, or it was discarded by the thief and sent to us by someone who found it. It's a bit of good news, which we haven't had for some time.'

And now the family was ready to move. They still had no intention of leaving Portugal without Madeleine and seemed to be settling in for at least the rest of the summer. 'We have confirmed our new accommodation and will be moving in the next few days,' said Gerry. 'We seem to have acquired a lot more stuff, particularly the twins, with lots of well-wishers sending them toys. We will be staying on in Portugal for the immediate future and we're determined to come home with Madeleine.'

The move, traumatic as it was in many ways was, however, a break with the immediate, crisis-driven past. It was a sign that the family was in some ways moving on: while they were still in Portugal, they were also trying to create a normal family home for the twins. It was two months now since Maddy had gone missing, and clearly, the issue had had to be addressed. Kate and Gerry had protected their two younger children from what had happened so far, but now they finally had to tell the twins Maddy was missing. The two sensibly sought advice from child psychologists about how to go about it and tackled the matter head on.

'We had some concerns about how to tell them, and it's a pretty private matter how we went about it, but I can tell you they are fine at the minute,' Gerry said. 'Our day starts pretty normal. Like most families with kids, we get them ready and take them to nursery, which allows us to do some work, and in the evenings it's pretty much back to family life.' But the work, of course, was doing all they could for Maddy to be found. As Kate herself said: 'It's pretty much like most family life, except during the day we have all the other things we need to do to campaign for Maddy's return.'

Global support was as strong as ever. The England rugby team was in Portugal for a training session for the forthcoming World Cup: for one practice session, they replaced their usual tops with t-shirts that said, 'Find Madeleine.' The team also met the couple. 'Everyone wants to do something, yet you feel so helpless,' said team member Martin Corry, who captained the McCann's local rugby team, the Leicester Tigers. 'All we can do is try to make sure that it is kept in the news.' The McCanns thanked the team: 'This generous gesture from the England squad, we hope, will remind sports fans that Madeleine is still missing,' they said.

But still, there were some who tried to take advantage of the situation. The couple were the subject of a second extortion attempt in early July, this time from an unemployed man in Holland, who had been demanding £1.35 million to reveal Maddy's whereabouts. Gerry had clearly had enough: 'This extortion attempt has caused Kate and I considerable distress,' he said. The man had sent six e-mails to the couple, which had been traced back to an Internet café and an unemployment office in Eindhoven: during questioning, he admitted making up the story. Of course, he had no actual information about Madeleine's whereabouts. Nor was he alone. Back in the UK, a woman was jailed in Cannock, Saffs, after faking a door-to-door collection for Maddy that was actually to fund her drug habit.

Briefly, it seemed as if the Portuguese police might actually be making some headway. Despite their failure to pin anything on him to date, Robert Murat's name suddenly re-entered the proceedings, with the police saying he was going to be brought in for questioning again. There was also some talk of others being involved. 'While there is only one official suspect so far, investigators have identified other people they believe were involved in the case and they are now being sought,' said a police source.

Murat still didn't speak, but his estranged wife Dawn did and was adamant her husband had done nothing wrong. 'Rob told me the police intend to talk to him again,' she said. 'It's worrying, of course, but there's nothing I can do about it. Hopefully, any new meeting with police will be to tell him he is no longer involved in their inquiries.'

In the event, the police quizzed him for ten hours to clarify details and apparent contradictions in his witness statements, but the fact remained that there was nothing concrete to link him to the case and no matching DNA evidence. 'He told me they are just going through everything again but he sounds well and I'm sure it's just a routine thing,' said Tuck Price. 'We have known all along, everyone has known, that Robert was going to have to be re-questioned to check the facts, but we have just never known when it was going to be. It has been a very surreal experience for him. He is holding up, but he wants it to be over. He wants to see his family in the UK, his daughter, as soon as arguido status is lifted. They will either come here or he will go there.'

Matters took a surprising – and given what was going to happen to the McCanns themselves – rather ominous turn, when three of the friends with whom they'd been holidaying flew back to Portugal to talk to the police at the same time that Murat was being questioned. Rachael Oldfield, 36, Russell O'Brien, 36, and Fiona Payne, 34, were all having dinner with the McCanns on the night Maddy vanished, and were called back to recall what had happened on the night. 'We are more than happy to help the police,' said Mrs Oldfield, speaking for the three of them. 'All of us want to do anything we can to help find Madeleine and reunite her with her loving parents.

I know Kate and Gerry are grateful to the Portuguese people for their prayers and tremendous support.'

In the event, Murat and the three friends came face to face. It was common procedure in Portugal for an official suspect to be confronted with people who might be able to challenge his alibi and in Murat's case, while he said he had been at home all evening with his mother, the other three all said they saw him. 'They have been brought together in the same building,' said Chief Inspector Sousa. 'They have been discussing some differences between the things they said about the night Madeleine disappeared.' But far from anything positive coming out of the meeting, the two sides just seemed to have been pushed even further apart, as was shortly to become clear.

Meanwhile, Gerry made a brief visit back to the UK to meet with police at a reception at London's Dorchester Hotel. He got a standing ovation on his entrance, but as a video of his daughter was played, he broke down. The poor man had shown unbelievable fortitude, but the long search and no results had clearly taken their toll.

The Suspect Fights Back

If Robert Murat is innocent of all charges – and it should be said that at the time of writing, there is not one shred of concrete evidence against him – then he is a very-much-maligned man. His reputation is in tatters and unless the mystery of what happened to Madeleine is ever fully resolved, then there will always be a cloud hanging over his name. The greatest victim in this whole sorry saga is, of course, Madeleine herself, followed by her parents and siblings; but Murat, too, has suffered and this became evident in a bizarre outburst shortly after the most recent police grilling. It was, at the very least, the sign of a man under almost unbearable stress.

'I have not thought about Gerry and Kate McCann or what they are going through because all I am bothered about is myself and what is going to happen to me, not them,' he said. 'I can't carry on living like this, no human being could. I am an innocent man. I am not a paedophile or any of the other things I have been called. I have done nothing wrong. I wake up with this nightmare every morning and I go to bed with it every night. This has had a terrible effect on my family, both here in Portugal and back in Britain. I am the only suspect and it could take years for them to release me from the investigation.

'I was questioned all last week, but it's far from certain what's going to happen. They have to find enough evidence to present a judge with a case, and it appears they do not have enough information to do that. If they let me go it will look like they have no idea and they do not want to do that. There is a huge difference in the mentality of the Portuguese police and detectives in the UK. When anything bad happens in Portugal, people disappear, they run and hide and now I understand why they do it. I have thought about it but it would not be fair on my family.

'The law here dates back to the days of fascism and it shows. I am putting my life at risk just by speaking like this. At the start of this, people were praying for the little girl to be found, but now those same people want me to be cleared. They are thinking about me and my nightmare. The attention is on me. I have a four-year-old daughter, but I will not be able to see her while all this is going on.

'My ex-wife Dawn also has a son who I have brought up like my own. Last year his lung collapsed and this year he needs to have another operation. It hurts me that I cannot be there for him. The police are just going over the same ground over and over again and I am not even allowed to tell my side of the story. It makes me so angry I want to punch something. Certain people think I should be in prison but the police obviously can't find enough evidence to do that, so why should I be made to live like this? I am in a corner and I cannot defend myself. I refuse to hide myself away from the world but my fate is in the hands of the police. I can see no light at the end of the tunnel.' Murat was clearly at the end of his tether, and judging by his words, it was hardly surprising that friends were concerned he was on the verge of a breakdown.

Meanwhile, the McCanns were endeavouring, as much as they could, to get on with their lives. Kate and the twins joined Gerry in Britain for a christening – it was the first time Kate had been back since Maddy was taken – in Skipton, Yorkshire. 'Saturday was an emotional day,' Kate said afterwards. 'We were reunited with family. Gerry and I wanted to be there, to take part and support our godchildren on one of the most important days of their lives. I am sure every mother in the world will understand it was heartbreaking for me to be with our family, yet not be with Madeleine.'

With the launch of the seventh and final Harry Potter novel, *Harry Potter and the Deathly Hallows*, its author JK Rowling joined in with the international search. She had already contributed to the fund to find Maddy and now, at her insistence, posters were to be displayed next to cash desks where the book was to be sold. The A3 posters could also be downloaded from the Internet: they had three pictures of Madeleine, with the main one highlighting the 'black flash' in her right eye, and read, 'If you have seen me please contact your local police agency.'

The McCanns, who said that *Harry Potter and the Philosopher's Stone* was one of Maddy's favourite films, were very touched. 'It's absolutely fantastic,' said Gerry. 'It is such a kind and huge gesture. JK Rowling was initially approached by one of our friends to see if she could do something to help raise awareness of Madeleine's disappearance. The English language version is being launched on Saturday and hopefully they will be doing it in different languages as well. We hope very much this will help us find Madeleine but also raise awareness of other missing children.'

The fund stood at £900,000, and it was helping to support the family while they stayed on in Portugal. Indeed, they would have been hard pressed to manage without it. 'We're going to need it,' said Madeleine's great-uncle Brian Kennedy. 'There are big bills coming in for things we've produced, for travel, for accommodation while Kate and Gerry are out there. They're not wealthy and there's no way we could carry on without it.'

There had been some criticism levelled at the McCanns to the effect that if they hadn't been doctors (i.e., professional people), they would never have received so much help. Brian was not impressed. 'It's true we have friends others may not have and we used them,' he said. 'We called in favours. Any parent, wherever they are, whatever they do, should get the same publicity as Madeleine has and if we can do anything through the fund for others then we will.'

The McCanns, of course, were still consumed by what was going on around them, but in other ways normality gradually began to return. In Rothley, the toys around the war memorial were being sent away to charities, the messages collected for the McCanns to read at a later date and the yellow ribbons were taken down. But for Gerry and Kate, there was no normality. 'We have got no plans to come home,' they said in a statement. 'We only want to return with Madeleine.'

Matters now appeared to have entered a stalemate. Robert Murat continued to be in the frame; news would emerge of a fresh and exciting lead, only for it all to die down again within days. There were fresh rumours of sightings and, at one stage, stories that Madeleine had been smuggled out of Portugal by boat. Gerry, by now on unpaid lead, continued to travel: the next destination was going to be the

United States, where he hoped to meet Laura Bush. 'Kate and I felt it was important to make this trip to America,' he said on his arrival. 'It's not that we think Madeleine is in the US. But it is predominantly a trip to speak to the top experts in the field of missing children.'

It was certainly a way of highlighting a problem that existed worldwide. Gerry met the US attorney general, Alberto Gonzales, at the State Department of Justice to discuss the Adam Walsh Child Protection and Safety Act, which Mr Gonzales had been instrumental in introducing the previous year. It followed years of campaigning by the parents of Adam Walsh, after their six-year-old had been snatched from a shopping mall in Florida and then murdered, twenty-five years ago.

'Mr Gonzales obviously played a pivotal role in the introduction of this bill,' said Gerry. 'It has brought about a lot of interesting changes to the way the US deals with offences towards children. It is something we are interested in looking into further.' The new law forced the expansion of the sex offenders register and imposed stiffer penalties for convictions; it also meant that paedophiles had to inform the authorities if they moved states, and the police had to alert the FBI within two hours of a child going missing.

Adam's parents, John and Reve, had campaigned

for a long time for this, and John had also helped found the National and International Centre for Missing and Exploited Children. Gerry visited the centre, which was covered with pictures of Maddy: 'I think I recognise that little girl,' he said. 'It's amazing, but it feels like everyone in the world is praying for Madeleine. It's very uplifting to hear stories of how children have been reunited with their parents, sometimes many years later.'

However, there was criticism mixed in amongst the good will. Gerry did indeed meet Laura Bush, but he also faced a grilling from American journalists about why the couple had left their children alone that night. It came at the same time unpleasant allegations about the couple and their friends started to emerge in the Portuguese press. The magazine *Sol* hinted that Gerry and Kate might be suspects in the inquiry, while accusing them and their friends of hiding behind a 'wall of silence.' Given how much publicity the McCanns had sought for their missing daughter, the accusation seemed nothing short of bizarre.

Meanwhile, Gerry was being quizzed on ABC's *Good Morning America*. 'We were dining fifty yards away and we could see the apartment from where we were,' he said. 'It's like we were sat in our back garden, albeit at the end of the garden. The kids were sound asleep and they were being checked regularly. We didn't think we needed a babysitter.

We are good parents and what we did felt perfectly reasonable at the time.'

He then appeared on CNN where he was asked about the possibility of being prosecuted for leaving the children alone. 'We have been assured by the authorities that what we did fell well within the boundaries of good parenting,' he said. 'Madeleine was targeted by a predator and we shouldn't have to worry about people getting into our homes and gardens and playgrounds. That is the real criminal act here.'

Afterwards, he was understandably a little irritated by having been pushed on the defensive. 'The real issue is that we should not have a constant fear of abduction of our children,' he said. 'What Kate and I did was at worst naïve and no one should forget that the real criminal is the predator who has taken a completely innocent child in such a premeditated fashion. It is this act that has wreaked havoc on our family and affected millions of other people.'

But it was all turning ugly. Calls for the McCanns to be prosecuted continued to mount in Portugal, while some really vicious comments were now being made. Horrifyingly, they found themselves at the centre of a hate campaign, while their local paper, the *Leicester Mercury*, had to remove its online message facility after unpleasant remarks about the couple appeared.

As if that were not enough, reports of what happened

when the McCanns friends came face to face with Robert Murat began to emerge. One of the women was said to have shouted, 'I know you were there. I would recognise you anywhere.' This, apparently, was a reference to the fact that Murat had a lazy left eye because of a detached retina.

Tuck Price spoke out. 'Robert found it traumatic,' he said. 'He could not understand how these people could sit there and accuse him of lying. It all seemed to revolve around them recognising his dodgy eye. It was dark. How could they have seen it? Besides that, he was not there anyway.'

The three-month anniversary of Madeleine's disappearance was marked by another spate of sightings, this time in Belgium, which again came to nothing. The repercussions of the case continued to spread: in Britain, InsureandGo, Britain's biggest direct travel insurance specialist, became the first insurer to offer cover against children going missing on holiday.

Kate and Gerry continued their almost superhuman efforts to keep Madeleine in the limelight. They travelled to Huelva, in southern Spain, where they spent three hours putting up missing posters throughout the city. And they managed to stay hopeful. 'There are moments when I fear the worst,' Kate said. 'I start panicking but I have to keep believing Madeleine is still alive. We have to remain hopeful. We love Madeleine very much and she knows that. As time goes on we feel stronger and we have felt very supported.'

But she was absolutely haunted by what had happened – unsurprisingly so. 'We're so desperately sorry,' she continued. 'Every hour now I question why I thought that was safe. Maybe it was because it was family friendly, because it felt so safe. That week, we had left them alone while we had dinner. There is no way on this planet I would take a risk, no matter how small, with my children. I love her and I'm a totally responsible parent and that's the only thing that keeps me going. You don't expect a predator to break in and take your daughter out of bed. I do feel regret. I've gone through all my life and said I would never want to have any regrets, but you can't not regret something like that.

'It could have happened under other circumstances and there would still be the regret. It wasn't like a decision we made. It was a matter of, "let's get the kids to sleep and then we'll have dinner." It wasn't a "shall I, shan't I?" thing. People have told us that we're the unluckiest people in the world and we are. That night runs over and over in my mind and I'm sure people will learn from our mistake, if you want to call it that. It is important not to lose sight of the fact we haven't committed a crime. Somebody has. Somebody's been there, somebody's been watching.'

At least the couple had each other. When really terrible events happen in families, they can either bring everyone closer together or force them further apart. In the McCanns' case, the former was true. 'As a couple, I think we're stronger than ever,' said Kate. 'We're feeling far from lucky at the moment, but we are lucky that we've got a strong relationship. We've got an equal partnership. We don't row; we've never rowed. We have communication, we talk a lot and that is vital at the moment. We have different strengths and have reached different stages at different points, but we each help each other. Gerry's way of coping is to keep busy and focused. He needs to feel like he's doing something. He's a very optimistic, positive person. I'm not, always. With a lot of the campaign stuff, he has done the talking. Sometimes I want to speak, but I can't. It's not natural for me. Gerry's used to having to speak at conferences and it's harder for me.'

Kate's strength was really remarkable. She came across as exactly what she was: a grieving mother who had suffered every parent's worst nightmare. And yet still she managed to be strong and to carry on. 'I'm equally involved,' she said. 'Every decision is mutual. When Gerry went to Washington, he rang me three or four times a day to ask me what I thought. Although I wasn't there in person, I knew hour by hour what was happening. His trip to the US was okay; it's funny what you manage to cope with. We knew it was a positive visit. It wasn't about Madeleine in particular.

We've learned a lot and become aware of the bigger issue. There are so many children out there, abducted children and sexually exploited children. Once you know all that, you can't turn a blind eye to it. It's not like I go around in a bubble, but I honestly did not realise the scale of this problem.' As she spoke, Kate was wearing a silver locket with a picture of Maddy: it was inscribed with the words, 'Tower of Strength.'

Meanwhile, the search continued. There were reports the kidnapper was working with an accomplice: nothing further emerged. What was left of Robert Murat's home, Casa Liliani, was dug up still further: nothing was found. However, one report surfaced that was to have a greater resonance: for the first time it was suggested that Maddy had been killed in the apartment. The finger of suspicion began to point to the McCann family and their friends. It was alleged that traces of Maddy's blood had been found in the apartment which had only finally come to light when a British sniffer dog was brought in: the Portuguese press reported that there were now suspicions there had been an 'accident' and 'forensic experts have revealed that somebody did try to erase the blood traces. The investigators are convinced that the blood belongs to Madeleine, but they are still holding back the detailed results of the tests until their suspicions are confirmed.'

Right from the start there was controversy over the findings, not least because Madeleine had now been missing for a full three months. Why on earth had the traces of blood not been found before? Countless people had been through the apartment since then, and given the amount of time that had elapsed, there could be any number of explanations as to why the blood was there. After all, Maddy could have cut her finger playing, and one of her parents could have mopped up after her. The Portuguese police came in for yet further criticism in the wake of the revelation.

'I am staggered that it has taken so long,' said ex-Surrey police detective Mark Williams-Thomas. 'This discovery should have been made on day one and if it proves to be significant, it will show just how inept the Portuguese police were at carrying out initial forensics tests. It is great that the British police have finally carried out a review but you have to ask why it has taken three months to happen.'

The Portuguese police were, not for the first time, on the defensive. 'These dogs are very highly trained animals' said a spokesman. 'We do not have anything like this in our country yet.'

The new evidence was uncovered by a team led by South Yorkshire police officer Martin Grime, one of the top sniffer-dog handlers in the world. Two spaniels were sent into the apartment, one a 'blood dog,' trained to locate traces of blood, and one a 'body dog,' trained to sniff out corpses. Both, according to the Portuguese press, detected something in the flat: traces of blood and the scent of a dead body. Tiny specks of blood, which were only visible under ultra-violet light, were found half way up the wall in Madeleine's bedroom: someone had appeared to have tried to wipe them off. DNA tests were carried out, comparing the blood to a strand of Madeleine's hair; it would take two weeks before the results could be announced.

This was the moment at which the investigation began to change direction. Despite further extensive searches of vehicles belonging to Robert Murat and his mother, absolutely no incriminating evidence had been found. The Portuguese police needed to make some headway, not least because they had come under such criticism in the international press. Unable to pin Madeleine's disappearance on Murat, and with all the other reported sightings coming to nothing, there was, they would seem to have believed, only one last place to turn. And that was towards the McCanns.

The mutterings that had been going on for weeks now rose to the surface: the McCanns and their friends were to be interviewed again. For Kate and Gerry, the pain must have been unimaginable: not only had they lost their little girl, but now they were being accused of harming her themselves. 'Kate and Gerry are well aware what these reports are inferring – that they or one of their close friends killed Madeleine, either deliberately or by accident,' said a source close to the couple. 'Gerry is absolutely livid about it all. It is complete nonsense. It is hurtful and untrue.'

Olegario Sousa denied that they were beginning to change their minds about the McCanns. 'The family are not suspects,' he said. 'This is the official position.'

But elsewhere a different story was emerging. The Portuguese newspaper *Diario de Noticias*, which had been following the proceedings with an informed eye, noted, 'Portuguese police have known for a month that Madeleine McCann was killed that night at the apartment, having definitely rejected the chance that she may have been kidnapped.' The McCanns, on the other hand, were still being told by the police that the assumption was that Madeleine might be alive.

The McCanns hired Renault Scenic was also tested for blood, while contradictory reports were flooding out from all quarters. Whispers said that Maddy's body had been dumped in the sea. Robert Murat looked set to be in the clear, but there was widespread (and justified) disgust about what was being said about the McCanns. 'I think there are some links coming from the police, but a lot of what I have read recently has been completely untrue,' said Rachael Oldfield, the recruitment consultant who had been on holiday with the McCanns and was dining with them the night Madeleine disappeared, and who herself has a one-year-old daughter.

'Whether a journalist has had a bit of information and made the rest up or the police are feeding some truth or untruths, I just don't know. It's very hurtful and it is all rather ludicrous. But it's difficult to defend ourselves because the investigation and everything in it is confidential. We don't want to jeopardise the investigation in any way, or Madeleine's life. We are a bit stuck, really.'

But it was not just the police who appeared to be changing their minds: the whole of the country did, too. The best explanation for this was that there was a kind of national embarrassment about it: first that the crime had been carried out on Portuguese soil, and second that the spotlight of the world was shining on it. Nor had the Portuguese police distinguished themselves. And so the wave of sympathy that had washed over the McCanns from the Portuguese began to ebb away.

Nowhere was this more noticeable than in the newspaper *Jornal De Noticias*. It adopted a tone of outright hostility: 'There are aspects that must still be clarified in all of this and there is a fundamental doubt as to whether everything took place as described by the English tourists,' it proclaimed. 'If their account of the monitoring of the children is to be believed, it would have been almost impossible to kidnap.'

Rachael Oldfield was horrified. 'I've read a timetable of what is supposed to have happened on the night and the timings are completely wrong,' she said. Other friends were equally nonplussed, but preferred not to speak out as Portuguese law presented a problem about doing so.

But no one was more appalled than the McCanns. 'We want to make it clear that, as far as we know, there is still absolutely no evidence that Madeleine has been seriously harmed, and Kate and I have to believe she is still alive,' he said. 'The Portuguese police have assured us on numerous occasions that they are looking for Madeleine and not a corpse. Of course all possibilities are being considered and the police have to be certain before eliminating any of the scenarios. It is absolutely right that we are subject to the same high standards of investigation as anyone else. Kate and I have, and will continue, to assist the police in every possible way. We hope there is a breakthrough very soon. In the meantime, the campaign to keep the public involved in the search for Madeleine continues. We are always trying to think of ideas that will reach people who may not have heard of Madeleine's disappearance.'

There were, right from the start, doubts about the turn the investigation was taking. It seemed all too convenient

The strain and despair start to take their toll on Kate McCann.

The church of Nossa Senhora da Luz (Our Lady of Light), where the McCann family sought constant solace after Maddy's disappearance.

After a tip-off in a letter, pollice start searching certain areas for clues as to Madeleine's whereabouts.

A relaxed and happy three-year-old Madeleine at her parents' home in Rothley.

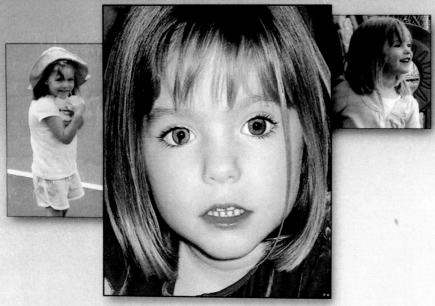

MISSING CHILD

Have you seen this child?

Madeleine McCann

If you have seen me,
please contact your local Police Agency!

The International Centre for Missing & Exploited Children
(ICMEC)
Is a leading global service agency working to protect the world's children
from exploitation and abduction.

www.icmec.org

www.findmadeleine.com

International Centre
FOR MISSING & EXPLOITED CHILDREN

Created by ICMEC in support of Find Madeleine Campaign

This page and facing page: posters have appeared all over the world asking for any information that might reunite Madeleine with her family.

HELP FIND OUR MADELEINE

PLEASE LOOK

IF YOU SEE HER
CONTACT YOUR LOCAL
POLICE NOW

www.findmadeleine.com/www.icmec.org

The McCanns finally arrive back in the UK; Gerry and Kate's stress is palpable.

The McCann's try to get back to living a 'normal' life – though as Kate stated 'How can it be normal without Madeleine?'

Thousand of soft toys and sympathy cards filled the town centre in the McCann's village of Rothley.

Madeleine's prayer

Where there is good in the world, let this good unite.

Where there is strength, let us be as giants in the face of darkness.

Where there is hope, let our hearts long for Madeleine's return.

that, just when it became apparent the police had yet to discover anything, the spotlight suddenly turned on the McCanns. And it seemed they had form. The case of Joana Cipriano cropped up again: the nine-year-old had vanished just seven miles from where Maddy disappeared three years previously, and her mother Leanor was now serving a sixteen-year sentence after confessing to her murder. But there were serious doubts as to whether she'd actually committed the crime, and her husband, Leandro Silva, made them clear. The police were trying to frame the McCanns, he said, to set them up for something they hadn't done. It was alleged that the confession was beaten out of Leanor. 'I am worried Kate will be framed for a crime she didn't commit, the way it happened to my wife,' he said.

Many other people, however, were not so sympathetic. There were suggestions the McCanns should leave Portugal. The Portuguese press was turning quite vicious. The man in the street wasn't much better. It was savagely hurtful.

But the McCanns stood firm. 'We will never go through anything worse than parting from Madeleine,' said Kate. 'We will not be leaving or be forced out. I am not prepared to be bullied into doing something I don't want to. We can cope with a lot and we still have a lot of strength, but this speculation and the actions of the Portuguese press have been hurtful, intrusive and disrespectful to our two other children. The press here has badly overstepped any reasonable line. The last week has been particularly difficult, but we want to focus on Madeleine, not us. We are a fairly ordinary couple and we really are in the most extraordinary circumstances but we have to do our best to find Madeleine. It is hard for us not knowing what has happened to Madeleine.'

But there were also reports that the local community was becoming less supportive, and, unsurprisingly, Robert Murat's lawyer led the charge. Francisco Pagarete insisted the locals wanted 'the bloody McCanns' to go home, and went on to accuse them of 'strange behaviour.' 'As a Portuguese person, I think it is strange that somebody would leave their kids,' he said. 'Then, after the first thing happened, they left their twins and went to see the Pope. It was like the McCanns on tour. When I was a small child my parents had me on a leash so I would not run away. Kids are like that. Incidents can happen. Maybe the poor child could open the door and got away. You would never leave them alone like that in a foreign country and go and have a drink. It is not a normal thing.

'People in Praia da Luz say, "These bloody McCanns should just go away and leave this town. They are giving it a bad name." Some people who live here will be happy when this whole circus goes away. People are talking about "those bloody McCanns" because they are getting annoyed about all the bad publicity about Praia da Luz. People are getting tired of it all. This used to be a quiet place and people have businesses to think of. They rent houses and it is a question of bad publicity. People are thinking this is not a safe place to bring their children and have cancelled holidays here.'

The one-hundredth day of Maddy's disappearance was a sombre time for the McCanns. Nor was any more headway being made. The Portuguese police had let it be known that they were now concentrating on a 'missing hour' between 9.05pm, when Gerry checked on the children, and 10.00pm, when Kate did likewise and found Madeleine was missing. Jane Tanner, one member of the group on holiday with the McCanns had told of a man walking away from the scene with a child wrapped in a blanket at about 9.30pm; an Irish ex-pat, meanwhile, made a sighting of a similar looking man and child heading towards the sea about twenty minutes later. The British sniffer dogs had traced something up to the sea, but at some point the trail had gone cold.

Despite the unpleasantness, however, fellow churchgoers warmly greeted the McCanns the next day when they attended a service themed '100 Days of Hope'. Prayers were said for Madeleine and all missing children. Meanwhile, Gerry's mother, Eileen McCann, hit out at the rumours the couple was involved in the disappearance of their child. 'It's very upsetting,' she said. 'Gerry called me the other night and told me the Portuguese police had changed their tactics during interviews. They won't give them any information now, but the idea of Kate or Gerry being involved is ridiculous. Kate and Gerry love those children more than they love themselves. The allegations are just obscene.'

To make matters worse, a second trace of blood was found in the flat, this time in Kate and Gerry's bedroom. The Portuguese police continued to obfuscate, speculate and did nothing to restore their damaged reputation. The search was still very much on.

I'm Really Just Going Through the Motions of Life

There was no getting around it: the case was a mess. Not only had no headway been made on the case, but Kate and Gerry's suffering had been worsened immeasurably by the finger of suspicion pointing at them and the vitriol coming from the Portuguese press. They remained shaken but resolute. 'When children have gone missing in the past, Holly Wells, Jessica Chapman and Sarah Payne, I've watched the news and thought, "That's my worst nightmare," said Kate. 'I had no idea how those mothers got through the day. But until you're in that situation, you can't even begin to imagine what it is that gets you out of bed and into the shower. I'm really just going through the motions of life hoping, every night when I go to bed, that this will be the last day I'll have to get through without her.'

Chief Inspector Olegario Sousa was not exactly holding out much hope. 'In the past few days, there have been some developments and clues have been found that could point to the possible death of the little child,' he said. 'We are waiting for lab results of the evidence collected. All lines of enquiry are open – but these lines are a little bit more interesting.'

The police interviewed Gerry and Kate; Kate was seen leaving the station in tears. Nor did the police have the courtesy to share their information about Madeleine being seriously harmed with the McCanns before they made it public. The pressure was almost unendurable: 'I've never liked uncertainty and this is the worst kind of limbo,' said Kate. 'Gerry and I have spoken about this and in our hearts of hearts we'd both rather know – even if knowing means we might have to face the terrible truth that Madeleine might be dead. You just have to go on. And it doesn't take the guilt away. Whenever I laugh with the twins or eat something nice it's always there in the back of my mind, "Madeleine would love this."'

A new and upsetting rumour was now doing the rounds: that the McCanns had given their children medication to make them sleep, which was why the twins not only slept through Madeleine's abduction, but didn't even wake up when the police arrived. A source close to the McCanns furiously denied it. 'They did not give the children sedatives that night,' he said. 'They have never given their children sedatives.'

The police seemed fixated on the idea. 'It is a remarkable aspect of the investigation,' said a source within the police force. 'Madeleine was asleep in a bed between the twins' cots, one on either side. They were just a few feet away, yet they never woke up. We had hoped officers could have discovered information from the young ones in a gentle way. It might have been possible that they had unearthed things children may even have tried to bury in their subconscious – things they never even thought they'd witnessed. But in this case there was nothing. The twins simply carried on sleeping, even through all the noise and confusion during the desperate search that followed.'

Friends of the McCanns pointed out that the children had had a long day in the sun, but the Portuguese police were not to be swayed. And a cynic could point out that implicating the McCanns was very convenient for the Portuguese police. Kate and Gerry were doctors and would have access to sedatives as well as the knowledge of how to use them. The police started asking local pharmacies if they'd sold any sedatives or insect sprays containing knockout drugs in the days before Maddy vanished. Increasingly, it looked as if they were intent on building a case against the McCanns.

Test results came back from the bloodstains found in the flat: they weren't Maddy's. This did not, however, stop the Portuguese press from claiming the police were pursuing a 'new line of inquiry' centering on the McCanns. Dark hints surfaced that witnesses might become suspects. The case grew nastier, and murkier, still.

There didn't even seem to be agreement within the ranks of the Portuguese police. Chief Inspector Sousa was now announcing to all and sundry that Maddy was probably dead and hinting at the involvement of the McCanns; Alipio Ribeiro, meanwhile, the head of the Policia Judiciaria, was forced to speak out in support of the McCanns. 'The parents have never, ever been suspects,' he said. 'The police should be discreet and keep quiet, though there is always someone who talks. Sometimes it is someone who knows nothing and just wants to be a protagonist. There has been a lot of speculation and if I denied everything erroneous that had been published I would have no time for anything else.'

By the middle of August, the couple conceded that they would soon have to return to Britain. Apart from anything else, they could not afford to stay in Portugal much longer. Contrary to earlier reports, they had not spent any of the money raised for Madeleine on their own living expenses: rather, they were paying for their £1,200 a month apartment themselves and given that both were now on unpaid leave, their resources were beginning to dwindle.

Indeed, one of the more unpleasant smears levelled at them was that they were using the fund unwisely. The opposite was the case. Only £67,000 had been spent, and that was used on travel expenses, accommodation to do with the search, stationery and administrative costs – not a great deal given the global nature of the search. 'As soon as a request does come, then everything will be done to support the family,' said fund spokeswoman Esther McVey. 'But all that has been asked for is money for the website and various other expenses to do with finding Madeleine. Everything is totally scrutinised because we know it could be a long-term search. We are just trying to make the money go as far as possible.'

Then there were the twins. They knew their sister was missing now, and that their parents were trying to find her, and they were also able to attend a crèche in Praia da Luz. But it wouldn't be good for them to stay in Portugal forever: increasingly it was felt that they would be better off at home. 'At home there is a strong support network with lots of friends and family around to help,' said a friend of the family. 'They know their home is in Leicestershire.'

The police continued to fail to distinguish themselves. In what looked suspiciously like a case of clutching at straws, they now shifted their attention to a member of one of the McCann's party, Russell O'Brien, a 36-year-old father of two. In what was becoming their standard way of operating, the allegations actually appeared in the Portuguese press, which claimed he was absent throughout much of the meal on the night Maddy went missing and that another Brit was shortly to be named as a suspect. Needless to say, no charges were ever actually brought, but Dr O'Brien, whose partner Jane Tanner was a key witness, was forced to defend himself. 'These reports in the Portuguese press are completely untrue and extremely hurtful,' the couple said in a statement. 'We have spoken to the police today and have been assured that our status as witnesses has not changed.'

But behind the scenes, another shift was taking place. The McCanns were advised not to leave Portugal just yet as a major breakthrough was about to occur, and at the same time another whispering campaign began. This one alleged that Madeleine was killed in the apartment, accidentally or otherwise, and was advocated by police officers Guilhermino Encarnacao and Goncalo Amaral, the police officer accused of beating a confession out of a mother in the earlier case of a missing child. 'Following a secret meeting between the most senior detectives, they are now considering the possibility that the little girl might have been killed accidentally,' said a police source. 'Abduction is no longer the main lead and police believe stronger theories have now emerged. It could be murder or it could be an accident – at the moment detectives are working on the latter theory. The apartment is the key – all the answers lie there, they say – but they are far from resolving what exactly happened and why the body disappeared.'

The McCanns were appalled at the way the case was moving, and were almost on the verge of legal action against a Portuguese television reporter, Sandra Felgueiras, over comments that seemed to hint that they'd murdered their child. Sandra hotly denied this. 'I never insinuated anything like that,' she said. 'I just said that the police were now looking at the possibility that Madeleine died at the apartment. This has been widely reported both in Portugal and the UK. I interviewed the McCanns two weeks ago and I asked them if there was any possibility that Madeleine suffered any kind of accident that could have made her bleed. My question was, "Did Madeleine at any stage bleed and could the blood samples correspond to her" and they did not answer this question. I have never in my life put anyone under suspicion, I just told viewers that police are investigating the possibility that Madeleine has died and that it is murder or an accident.'

In the event, and probably wisely, the McCanns decided not to sue. It would have added yet another level of complexity to a case that was already so mired in controversy and so utterly muddied that no one, least of all the police, seemed to have any real idea what was going on. The McCanns stood in the middle of it all, in the very eye of the storm, battered and buffeted from all sides, and yet still clinging to the hope that Maddy was alive. It was a dreadful thing to have to endure.

And there was still a good case to be made that Madeleine had been abducted. If she was, she had almost certainly been taken between 9.05pm and 9.15pm. (9.05pm was when Gerry last checked on the children and 9.15pm was when Jane Tanner spotted a man walking away from the Ocean Club resort carrying a child.) The friend who checked at 9.30pm merely listened at the door rather than going in to the room. 'It could not have been anything other than abduction,' said a source close to the family. 'There is no doubt in anybody's mind that the girl Jane Tanner saw being carried away was Madeleine.' Kate and Gerry, meanwhile, remained convinced Maddy was being held in Spain.

But the rumours were now getting out of control. The Portuguese press had accused the McCanns of everything from being involved in wife swapping to forging Maddy's birth certificate, and so it was only a matter of time before they went the whole hog and accused them of murder. And indeed, that is just what happened next. Under the headline 'Policia Judiciaria believe parents killed Maddy', the magazine *Tal & Qual* revealed that the latest theory was that Kate and Gerry had accidentally killed their daughter by giving her an overdose of sedatives to help her to sleep. No matter that there wasn't a shred of evidence to support this: in their desperation to pin the blame on someone, only the McCanns were left.

And it was pretty ugly stuff. 'For the PJ investigators who analysed the disappearance of Madeleine McCann, the responsibility of the parents in the death of the little girl is practically a certainty,' *Tal & Qual* wrote. 'The information came from sources close to the investigation who believed everything happened in an accidental manner, not adding what could have happened. However, the hypothesis that she could have died accidentally in a drug overdose cannot be put aside.'

Gerry was beside himself. 'It is just so absurd, it is just not credible,' he said. 'It's incredibly hurtful and incredibly untrue. It comes down to: is it papers writing that or is it actually rumours that have been said? Without anything else, what that implies is that we somehow did it, we did it together, managed to dispose of Madeleine without a car, without anything, the whole group was involved, there must have been other people involved. Even if somebody could think that, there is just absolutely no evidence pointing in that direction.'

Chief Inspector Olegario Sousa reiterated that the couple were not suspects, but now it was only a matter of time before the official position was reversed on that. And the stress was taking its toll. Towards the end of August, Gerry caused uproar when he stormed out of a television interview with Spain's Channel Five news programme *La Noria*, when he was asked about blood spatters on the wall. A clearly shaken Kate was left to face the cameras alone: 'It's the pressure, don't worry, it's very frustrating,' she said. 'The whole world asks about the investigation and we can't talk about it. We would like to talk but we cannot talk, you know?' Indeed, Portuguese law was preventing them from doing so, but that didn't stop the host of the show asking the resident studio panel, 'It's not because of remorse, is it?'

The McCanns made another, desperate appeal: 'It's not too late to do the right thing,' they said in a message made public to the world. Rather heartbreakingly, it emerged that the twins still sometimes set a place for Maddy at the dinner table and urged their parents to hold food back for her in case she was hungry when she got home. But the tide of public opinion had well and truly turned – in Portugal, at least: websites that had originally been set up to help the couple now carried horrible slurs against them. They were even, bizarrely, criticised for telling the twins Maddy had been taken away, as if the twins weren't going to notice at some point that their sister was missing.

The official naming of the parents as suspects came a step closer in early September, just after the four-month anniversary of Maddy's disappearance. Kate was taken in for five hours' questioning, while reports surfaced that the 'smell of death' had been found in Kate's clothes and on a cuddly toy. 'Kate is terrified she is being set up,' said a friend. 'This has been the worst week for them since Madeleine vanished, and we're not through it yet. They have been very nervous all week. They had built themselves up to go home and now they have had to put those plans on hold.'

Finally the day came that everyone now knew was inevitable. On 7 September, the Portuguese police finally named Kate as an 'arguida', or official suspect. Gerry was named likewise shortly afterwards. It finally proved too much: just over four months after Maddy went missing, and two days after the parents were named as suspects, the McCann family flew back to Britain. Enough was enough. They had endured vilification and abuse on the top of the disappearance of their much-loved child: it really was time to come home.

The Portuguese police now had eighteen months to decide whether to charge them; the McCanns, meanwhile, had to sign an undertaking saying that they would return to Portugal if required. But having to leave without Maddy must have been unbearable. However, the search was still very much on. 'While we are returning to the UK, it does not mean we are giving up the search for Madeleine,' said

Gerry, his voice quivering with emotion, shortly after arriving at East Midlands Airport. 'As parents, we cannot give up on our daughter until we know what has happened. We have to keep doing everything we can to find her.'

After arriving back in Rothley, the family stayed hidden from view, although a doctor was seen to arrive and stay for an hour, prompting fresh concerns about Kate's health. She had appeared increasingly gaunt and exhausted – unsurprisingly, given the pressure she was under – and their community was eager to give them messages of support. 'As a village, we are very much behind the McCanns,' said Percy Hartshorn, chairman of Rothley Parish Council. 'They are back home now in familiar surroundings and we will do everything we can to give them the support they need.'

But the strain did not let up. The McCanns were barely back on British soil before reports surfaced in Portugal that Maddy's DNA had been found in a car they hired twenty-five days after she had vanished. 'Biological fluids' were found 'underneath the upholstery of the boot' claimed the Portuguese police. If, and it was a big if, this was really the case, it could have had any number of explanations, not least that Maddy's DNA was on the toys the family carried around. But the latest, utterly unbelievable, theory was this: Kate killed Maddy (by giving her an overdose, or slapping or shaking her) while Gerry played tennis or swam; she con-

144

fessed all to Gerry; he helped her hide the body; and then they disposed of it the best part of a month later using the hire car. And this, mark you, in the Portuguese heat, which would have accelerated decomposition, under the eyes of the world's media. To say this was clutching at straws was to give it a gravity it didn't deserve.

The family thought so, too, and lost no time in saying so. It was 'unbelievable' that Kate and Gerry had been named as suspects said Philomena McCann. 'The way the Portuguese have turned this investigation round, and they are no longer looking for a live child, they are assuming on spurious evidence that Madeleine is now dead, well, we don't agree with that in any shape or form,' they said. 'We want the investigation changed round to look for Madeleine alive, as we reckon she is. Kate and Gerry have been a thorn in their sides for a long time. What better than to cast them as villains? No-one believes the Portuguese police.'

She was right. Unsurprisingly, given the way they had been treated, the McCanns consulted Michael Caplan, QC, an expert in extradition law: even if the Portuguese had no real case against them, it was still conceivable they would be dragged back to be tormented in lieu of anyone else. Indeed, the latest reports coming out of Praia da Luz said that a mass of Maddy's hair had been found in the boot of the hire car. The 'body fluid' was said to be that of a decomposing body, but the Portuguese police had yet to come up with a reason that there was no accompanying smell. This would have been mid-June, in the searing heat.

Provoked beyond endurance, the McCanns finally hit back. It was difficult for them to speak directly – though Gerry was maintaining his Internet blog – but clearly, and understandably, they could take it no more. 'The legitimate question to ask the Portuguese police is, "Where is the body? Where is the evidence that Madeleine is dead?" We have got no idea,' a friend of the family said.

The Portuguese police expressed hurt surprise. 'It seems remarkable that just days after the McCanns were saying they thought Madeleine was still alive and missing, now they're talking about a body,' said a source. 'I don't know if this is really the McCanns speaking or just one of the people working on their publicity campaign, but it is not the kind of comment to impress a team of detectives who think you're guilty.' The fact that the team had shown itself incapable of detecting its way out of a paper bag was neither here nor there: the comments were simply risible.

The McCanns' Portuguese lawyer, Carlos Pinto de Abreu, certainly thought so. 'It is more appropriate to break down the patience of a believer and the reputation of an innocent man than to identify those responsible,' he said scathingly. Meanwhile, John McCann, Gerry's brother, pointed out that, as usual, there was no evidence whatsoever to support the latest allegations. 'There is so much speculation going on as to what the Portuguese police have,' he said. 'If they have got something that suggests Madeleine really is dead, then for goodness sake tell the family, who have the strongest feeling for this.'

Brian Healy, Kate's father, was equally appalled. 'There is no way in a month of Sundays that Kate would hurt her little girl,' he said. 'It is disgraceful to say she would, it is lies and I think something is going on to smear her. Kate it totally innocent and it hurts me so much to hear those claims.'

Another of the reports centred on Kate's diary. The police had made a big fuss about this, saying that she had recorded that she found it hard to control the children, and that she was at her wits end because Gerry didn't help. Brian was pretty scornful about this, too. 'Not in a million years did she fight to control Madeleine,' he said. 'It is nonsense. And as for Gerry not doing anything for the kids – he baths them, he plays with them, he does everything for them. The idea that Portuguese detectives are looking at my daughter's most personal thoughts and taking them out of context and leaking them to the papers is terrible. Kate and Gerry are scared people and they should not be. They are two good people who have done nothing wrong.'

If anyone should be in any doubt as to the competence of the Portuguese police, it was only now, well into September, that they decided to impound the car. They had, in fact, given it back to the McCanns after searching it, and when the McCanns returned to Britain, they left it in the safe-keeping of a friend. When the police finally called it in, hire car firm Budget spent twenty-four hours trying to locate it. Unsurprisingly, at this stage the McCanns decided they would carry out their own forensic tests.

And John McCann pointed out that he and some of the other relatives had driven the car. 'Does that mean we are suspects?' he queried. 'There are too many rumours about what so-called forensics show. The investigation is off-track.'

And still details continued to leak out. The latest was that Madeleine had 'definitely' had an overdose of sleeping pills as witnessed by forensic traces from the body (though this was not backed up by any actual evidence). However, it is a mark of how successful the Portuguese had been in casting doubt on the McCanns that several millionaire backers of the 'Find Madeleine' fund now made it clear that they would not countenance having the money used for the couple's legal defence. Eyewitnesses who had been around them when it all began expressed the view that it was simply impossible to believe that the McCanns had anything to do with it: a lot of mud had been thrown, however, and some of it had stuck.

But where was the body? The usual avalanche of rumour and innuendo emerged: it was put in a bag of stones, dumped in the sea and is lost forever, said the Portuguese police, who had suddenly and somewhat belatedly realised that if they didn't actually have a body, the case against the McCanns might well not stand up. But they would have had to do this under the full glare of the media spotlight, and not even the Inspector Clouseaus of Praia da Luz had yet managed to come up with an explanation as to how they managed to do that. That much was made apparent when the police finally admitted that only a confession from the McCanns would ever gain a conviction. The rest of it was sheer speculation, not fact.

Unsurprisingly, the DNA in the car turned out to be too insubstantial to bring any sort of case. The police admitted as much, while blaming the fact that they couldn't work out the full sequence of events from 2.00pm to 10.00pm for their cluelessness. 'There are a lot of clues, signs and indications, but without more elements it's impossible for us to determine what happened in those vital hours,' said a police source. 'Even if the blood and traces gathered in the car or the apartment were confirmed to correspond one hundred per cent to the little girl's DNA, that wouldn't prove anything. Those elements could only confirm, and at the moment we don't even have that, that the little girl was in the apartment, which is plainly obvious, and in the car. In either of the cases, nothing would prove homicide, just that the body of the little girl had been transferred in the vehicle. We don't know if Madeleine is dead and, if she is, how it happened. Was she strangled? Could she have been beaten? They are all questions only the parents could clarify in an eventual confession.' And this, mark you, was from one of the men involved.

If the Portuguese police themselves were able to pick apart their investigation as easily as this, it was hardly surprising the rest of the world could, too. And on occasion, it almost looked as if they were making it up as they went along. Concerns arose, out of the blue, about the car's 'high mileage' (and this is the car that wasn't impounded after it was searched), after which it was declared that Madeleine's body could have been buried at Fatima, one of the holiest shrines of the Catholic Church. Nothing came of this line of inquiry. Various 'pet ovens' – places for cremating pets – were reported to have been searched a couple of months earlier at a business called Creon Starlight, run by a Dutchman near the town of Monchique, but again, no traces of Madeleine were to be found.

Kate and Gerry, meanwhile, began planning another

huge poster campaign across Europe to emphasise the fact that there was still no trace of their missing child.

In mid-September, the body of a five-year-old girl who had been linked to Maddy's disappearance was found in a forest in Switzerland. Ylenia Llenard was snatched from a swimming pool in Appenzell on 31 July: because of the obvious similarity between the two cases, the McCanns were shown a photograph of the missing child. The man suspected of kidnapping her was Urs Von Aesch, 67, who had shot himself on the day she went missing. But there, too, nothing further came of it.

The Portuguese police then came up with their next theory: that the McCanns had 'confessed' to two priests that they had killed their daughter. The two were the Catholic priest Father Jose Manuel Pacheco and a Canadian-born Anglican priest Haynes Hubbard, to whom both the McCanns had become close, and both of who were scathing in their assessment of the Portuguese police. 'The police have to find Madeleine,' said Haynes, who had two young children who had been playmates for the twins. 'We don't know if she is, in fact, dead. They won't find anything here. There is no indication the little girl is dead. She's waiting to be brought home to mum and dad.' It seemed the police were chasing up yet another blind alley.

The general disarray surrounding the proceedings was

forcefully brought home when Luis Bilro Verao, General Prosecutor for the district of Evora, said the McCanns would not face questioning again. 'The police have not collected any elements of proof since the McCanns were made arguidos on 7 September that justified new questioning,' he said. Nor did their bail conditions need to be changed, which meant they could stay at home in Leicestershire.

In the light of all of this, it was hardly surprising that the McCanns felt they had to take matters into their own hands. They decided to hire Control Risks Group, one of the UK's largest private security firms, which was known to employ ex-SAS men to see if they could get any further leads. It was also a world leader in hostage negotiations. Described as a 'shadowy, Le Carreesque outfit', it was staffed by former M16 and police officers, and had been set up in 1975 as a specialist consultancy by insurance broker Hogg Robinson after the threat of kidnapping of world business leaders increased sharply, especially in South America. Since its inception, it had helped to resolve more than one thousand cases.

Lurid headlines appeared in the Portuguese press: the police had been told to 'find the body or the McCanns will escape.' Given that the McCanns had just employed some of the most experienced people in the world to find their daughter, this appeared to be yet more posturing and, indeed, the legal community in Portugal said as much. According to Portugal's most senior prosecutor, Antonio Cluny, charges were now very unlikely. 'There is no confession and according to what has been made public, the evidence gathered until now keeps all leads open, from abduction to homicide, or at least to a simple accident,' he said.

Even so, it was a dreadful burden for the McCanns to bear. They were aware that unless Maddy was found, their own names would never be totally in the clear, as there would always be people who believed they had something to do with it. 'If no body is found and they are not charged and their status falls away, then they'll have this hanging over their heads,' said a source close to their lawyers. 'But that's unacceptable because they are innocent. Why should they have this stain on their characters? This would be the worst-case scenario, because nobody, least of all them, will ever know what's happened. The suggestion that they have to face justice, or escape justice, is loaded with assumptions of guilt.' To some people, perhaps, but to the vast majority of observers, the police had just made the McCanns' burden even harder to bear.

'We Know They Use Us at Times'

With the police search going nowhere, attention returned to an event that had so far received scant coverage: the pet crematorium on a run down farm near Monchique, less than twenty miles from Praia da Luz. The company, called Creon Starlight, was run by a Dutchman, Eef Hoos, who had previously spent almost eight years in prison for planting bombs in the Netherlands. The theory was, of course, that this is how the McCanns had got rid of the body and it was as ludicrous and farfetched as anything else the Portuguese police had come up with so far.

Nonetheless, they had taken Hoos in for questioning, repeatedly asking him if he'd ever met the McCanns. He was vehement in his denials. 'I can swear I had nothing to do with that girl's disappearance,' he said, as the police sealed off two furnaces on his farm. 'They were asking me about the McCann case. They asked me if I had anything to do with her disappearance and asked if I had spoken with the parents of Madeleine McCann. The police asked me three times if I had spoken to the parents. I said I had not spoken to the parents, but the other guy said he had heard that I had spoken to the parents of the girl. Naturally, I told them I knew nothing about it. I can swear I had nothing to do with that girl's disappearance.'

As usual, it was a case of the Portuguese police coming up with a theory and then trying to bend the facts to fit in with the case. The fact that Hoos was having an eye operation on 3 May, the day of Maddy's disappearance, was neither here nor there. His actual business was debt collecting and he ran the crematorium as a service for neighbours, he explained, but still the police wouldn't give up. A Polish couple had visited him recently with a large bag, asking for it to be incinerated: did he know what was in it? The fact that Hoos had checked and found it to be, as the couple had said, a Labrador, did not deter them.

Of course, Hoos was a bit odd, which made him a convenient person to drag into the whole affair. He had come to Portugal nine years previously, ironically for the piece and quiet of the place, and lived in a large two-storey villa guarded by two dogs. He said that he'd travelled to Russia and China as part of his debt collecting business, and incinerated animals as a sideline, mainly family pets but also road kill. Because of his previous conviction in Holland, the Portuguese police were already aware of him: 'The police said to me, "You have a very bad name." I am the biggest bomb maker in the world,' he said. But that didn't mean that he had anything to do with the case of Madeleine McCann and, indeed, nothing more came to light.

The McCanns, despairing of what was being said about them, offered to take a lie detector test. 'Taking a test would surely convince everyone once and for all of their innocence,' said a source close to the family. 'That would allow people to focus fully on the search for Madeleine and forget about the distraction of the ridiculous police investigation targeting Gerry and Kate.' Meanwhile, they were forced to hire Rogerio Alves to their defence team. Alves was one of the most senior lawyers in Portugal, president of the Portuguese Bar and an eminent attorney. He joined Carlos Pinto de Abreu as the couple's lawyers and in mid-September flew to London to discuss developments with the McCanns.

Friends of the couple were increasingly angry about what was going on. One, who was dining with them on the night Maddy went missing, pointed out quite how ludicrous the whole line of attack had become. 'It is farcical that detectives could even make Kate and Gerry suspects without speaking to witnesses at the time,' she said. 'Throughout all of this the police have never come back and asked eyewitnesses whether the McCanns could be faking it. There is no way they can charge them without speaking to the friends.

It's a farce. They were so distressed and distraught there is no way anybody could act like that. Even in a movie, nobody could fake it like that. Their suffering was completely real.'

And it was still ongoing. Back at home now, reminders of their missing daughter surrounded them: 'There are constant reminders of her all around them,' said a friend. 'There is the bedroom, her toys, her belongings. There are pictures of her all over the walls.'

The couple's spokesman Clarence Mitchell revealed, however, that they were trying to restore some normality to their lives, especially for the sake of the twins. 'Sean and Amelie can have a relatively normal life – of course it's not normal, but it's getting there slowly,' he said. 'If you spent any time with the McCanns as a family, you would know – on a human level, for one thing – that they haven't done it. The house is full of love for the children. They have not harmed Madeleine – let alone killed her, let alone disposed of her. In the middle of this people forget that this is a family potentially facing bereavement, but are still in that awful limbo of not knowing what's happened to their daughter.'

There had always been doubts about what exactly Kate had said on the dreadful night that Madeleine disappeared, but now a nanny, Charlotte Pennington, who worked for the Ocean Club complex tried to shed light on the matter. Various witnesses had separately heard Kate yell, 'She's gone,' or, 'They've taken her', and now it appeared it might well have been both. Kate, said Charlotte, was a 'broken woman.' 'We are trained to deal with people in this kind of situation, but she was just inconsolable,' she went on. 'I was in the apartment less than five minutes after they found Madeleine had gone. When we were coming out we saw Kate and she was screaming, "They've taken her, they've taken her." It might not have been the first thing she said, but she definitely said it.' But whatever she'd said, Kate was quite clearly distraught.

There had been sightings of one sort or another ever since Maddy had gone missing, but now one came to light that initially seemed extremely credible: she was again thought to have been seen in Morocco. Control Risks Group was sent in to investigate. Meanwhile, it was revealed that the person behind the scenes helping the McCanns was Brian Kennedy, a double-glazing tycoon who had made a £250 million fortune. Brian, whose company was called Latium, had not had any previous contact with the family, but was said to have offered to help when he learned they would not be able to call on the 'Find Madeleine' fund for their legal fees, and might instead have to sell their home to cover their costs.

'In light of the quite incredible accusations against Kate

and Gerry McCann, which are clearly exacerbating their emotional torture, I felt compelled to offer, along with other like-minded businessmen, financial support and the full logistical support of the Latium team,' he said. 'That support is principally our in-house lawyer Ed Smethurst and Clarence Mitchell. This will relieve the McCanns of the daily pressure of co-ordinating the legal teams that will expedite the clearing of Gerry and Kate's names, allowing all parties to focus on finding Madeleine.'

A rare moment of lightness came when details of Kate's light-hearted past as a student emerged. A decade and a half previously, when the then-Kate Healy was studying at Dundee University, it turned out that she was called 'Hot Lips Healy' because of her resemblance to Margaret 'Hot Lips' Houlihan, played by Loretta Swit in the long-running TV comedy M*A*S*H.

Her 1992 college yearbook came to light: she was, apparently, 'renowned for alcoholic binges and some "dance till you drop" nocturnal activities'. She was very popular, said a former friend who is now a doctor. 'Kate was great fun, always up for a laugh and a party,' he continued. 'She was certainly more interested in going to the pub than she was in her studies, although she seemed to pass her exams with ease.'

Her entry read: 'Kate "Scouser" Healey-chops "ferried"

over from Merseyside fives years ago and rapidly became the most prominent member of the H.G. Girlies. Renowned for frequently indulging in alcoholic binges and "dance till you drop" nocturnal activities, she immediately led the rest of her fellow colleagues astray. "Hot Lips" Healey maintained a consistent Friday night appearance in the Union throughout the whole of first year.'

A further indication of what a mess the proceedings had become came when Chief Inspector Sousa suddenly and dramatically announced that he would no longer be acting as a police spokesman. It wasn't long before the reason for this very public resignation came to light. It was becoming clear that all the numerous leaks from the police, which had led to such dreadful headlines for the McCanns in recent weeks, had been made specifically in order to get them to make a confession – and it hadn't worked. And not only that, but the leaks themselves were based on completely spurious information. There was no case against the McCanns as such: the police had merely been trying to manufacture one by dishing dirt they didn't actually have.

'He has told me he has always worried that the evidence against the McCanns was weak,' said one former policeman, who knew Sousa. 'He was worried it would not bear scrutiny. He told me he felt caught in the middle of a propaganda war between his colleagues and the McCanns.'

One of the Portuguese journalists who had been cover-ing the story said as much. 'Some Portuguese journalists were fairly convinced the so-called evidence passed on to them by police was nowhere near as concrete as their sources suggested,' said Jose Lugios, a freelance journalist who was based in the area. 'The way it works here is that we can't get official police comments so we have to rely on tip-offs from them. We know they use us at times ... as they did when they drip-fed us snippets that might exert enough pressure on the McCanns to confess. But that's the strange way it works. It's the only way we can get crime stories.'

In case anyone was left in any doubt as to what was be-hind it all, another police officer from a neighbouring force spoke out. 'The Portimao police were definitely furious that they were depicted as bumbling and ineffectual,' he said. 'They were especially furious about stories of their long, drunken lunches and their alleged willingness to force a confession to cover their ineffectual investigations. They know they made mistakes – a whole catalogue – from fail-ing to secure the crime scene, to leaving the border with Spain open for a further twelve hours after Madeleine van-ished, to returning the hire car to the McCanns despite having found allegedly incriminating evidence inside. But their own press would never write critically of them – they needed to keep the relationship sweet. It was a slap in the face and a shock when the British press not only branded them inept but heaped ridicule upon them, too.'

In the middle of this war of words, the fact that Maddy was still missing was in danger of getting lost. No one, of course, was more aware of that than the McCanns themselves and they were extremely keen to shift the focus of attention back where it belonged. 'Kate and I have been very busy with our legal advisers as we want to be eliminated from the inquiry as soon as possible and start concentrating wholeheartedly again on the search for our daughter,' said Gerry. We are very confident this will happen when all the facts are presented together.'

But they were being hampered at every turn. In late September, it was reported that there had been a sighting of Maddy in Morocco, a sighting that was at first taken extremely seriously. A picture was published of what looked from a distance like a gang of Moroccans carrying a small, blonde child, who appeared a little distressed. She was spotted by a Spanish couple, the Torres, in Zinat, who were so struck by the likeness that they took a photo of her from their car window on their mobile phone, and e-mailed it to the police in their hometown of Albecete, in southeast Spain. The photograph was quickly sent on to the McCanns' London lawyers.

It was not a clear picture, and had been taken from about

two hundred metres away, but there certainly was a slight resemblance to Madeleine. Clara Torres certainly thought so. 'I was taking photos of everything we saw, and we saw a group of people and took a photo,' she told the Spanish radio station COPE. 'As soon as I did we were struck by the little girl, who was very blonde. We said the name of the girl, but we couldn't believe it could be her. When we arrived back in Spain we downloaded the photographs on to our computer. Then we heard on the news that there were various people who said they had seen Madeleine in Morocco. I ran to the computer and started to amplify the photo and when we saw it we realised, yes, it could be her. It sent shivers down my spine.'

Nor was it the first time there had been a sighting of Madeleine in Morocco. Isabel Gonzales, a Spanish tourist, was certain that she'd seen Maddy in the remote town of Zaio, months previously. 'I am totally convinced I saw Madeleine with a Muslim woman crossing the street in Zaio towards the end of May,' she said. 'I saw her face clearly from just a few yards and immediately thought, "That's Madeleine!" The woman was acting strangely, hiding her face from the traffic, which struck me as odd.

'I screamed at my husband for him to stop the car so we could get to the woman and challenge her. But by the time we stopped and jumped out, the woman and the girl had disappeared. My husband and I began searching the streets, asking everyone if they had seen a woman with a small blonde girl. We went in every shop and cafe, but the people of the town just weren't interested in helping. I was in tears, distraught, and I felt totally powerless. I am a mother so I can imagine what Madeleine's parents must be going through.

'We reported the incident to the police later that day but they just weren't interested. So the next day we took some photos of Madeleine from the newspapers and drove back to the town. We asked everyone we met, showing them the photo, but we just got blank faces in return. Nobody in the area seems to care. We also had some photos of the spot where we saw the girl and took these to the police to help their investigation. But they have failed completely to investigate our sighting.

'The town is very isolated and the area around it is like a wilderness, with hundreds of houses dotted around the outskirts where a small girl could be hidden away. The girl I saw was blonde, with pale skin, whereas everyone else in the area is dark-skinned and dark-haired. A gust of wind blew her hat up as she crossed the road in front of us and I saw her little face looking scared and worried. As a mother I feel I have to do everything I can to help.

'The woman was short and stocky, and wearing a black

headscarf and brown full length Arabic dress. She was walking very fast across the road, not even checking for the oncoming traffic.' The Spanish police, however, did nothing, and so Isabel got in touch with their Portuguese counterparts. They, however, were also no help. 'They said to me, "It can't be Madeleine, we believe she's dead",' said Isabel. 'I can't imagine how many other leads they might have just ignored. I don't want the publicity but I am so convinced I saw Madeleine that I will do anything to help.'

It looked to be the most promising lead in the case so far but sadly, almost immediately turned out to be false. The little girl was swiftly tracked down: she turned out to be Bushra Binhisa, the five-year-old daughter of Hamid Binhisa, a farmer in the Rif mountains of northern Morocco. 'Bushra is my little girl,' said Hamid, speaking through an interpreter. 'She is not Madeleine. I do feel sorry for her parents; I hope they find Madeleine.'

His wife, Hafida, who had been carrying the little girl, was equally sympathetic, saying her heart went out to the McCanns. 'Even in this remote backwater people have heard of Madeleine McCann,' she said.

And the local townsfolk, while expressing how sorry they were about Madeleine, were also a little bemused that the mistake could have been made. 'We are all shocked that people thought Bushra was Madeleine,' said Mustafa Hadid, a friend of the Binhisas. 'She does have a resemblance, but blonde and red-haired children are not that rare in this part of Morocco.'

Nor, in a community this size, could Madeleine have been hidden for long. 'We've heard of Madeleine,' said a petrol station attendant in the town. 'But we don't get many British people coming through here. If she was here then everybody would have known about it and it would have been impossible to keep it a secret. We have seen her parents on the news and we feel upset for them. We hope she is found soon. I don't think any people here would have taken her.'

But who did? As the Portuguese police – or indeed, anyone – failed to make headway in the search for Maddy, it was suggested that Britain use its network of spy satellites to try to find out what had happened to the little girl. After all, there was satellite and aerial footage –to say nothing of monitored Internet access – that might yield up something, according to Professor Anthony Glees, Director of Brunel University's Centre for Intelligence and Security Studies. He believed that Britain's Joint Air Reconnaissance Intelligence Centre (Jaric) and spy headquarters GCHQ might be able to provide a clue towards solving the mystery, to say nothing of clearing the McCanns' name. There would be a lot of imagery from the area as the Iberian coast was of strategic military importance: it was where people crossed from North Africa into Europe.

'I've spoken to some people involved in these areas and they would be willing to do it,' he said. 'There's no reason why it couldn't be done but they would have to be ordered by the Prime Minister or Defence Secretary. Jaric is a world leader in analysing CCTV, aerial and satellite imagery collected from all over the globe. It should be ordered to overfly Praia da Luz immediately and collect any aerial imagery of it that can be found, dating back to 2 May 2007, as well as any images that may be extant.

'It should also be instructed to examine any satellite images of the target zone after 2 May. It is perfectly possible that the European Commission's satellites that track fishing boats may also be able to shed light on Madeleine's fate. If, God forbid, her body has been buried they could help identify spots where it is.'

The technology could also uncover a paedophile ring. 'GCHQ has a huge archive of email traffic which it does not look at unless ordered to by the Government,' he said. 'If they were tasked to do it, I've been told they wouldn't have a problem with it. Paedophiles make a lot of 'noise' on the web so they could be identified.'

It would certainly help the McCanns if their names were to be cleared. Even in Britain, people were voicing doubts as to whether they may have played a part in Maddy's disappearance, prompting the tycoon Sir Richard Branson to speak up in their defense. He had already donated £100,000 to the search, and now he gave an exclusive interview to the *Daily Express*, voicing his dismay as to what was happening. 'I don't know what you can say to a couple torn apart by grief like that,' he said. 'They're getting stronger. I was motivated to help them after a public poll in a newspaper recently showed that Britain was turning against them. I couldn't bear to see that happen. But now it looks like the tide is turning and they are bearing up much better. There's nothing worse than being blamed and punished for something that is not your fault. People commit suicide over such accusations. It's tragic.'

Back in Portugal, the search continued. The Portuguese police had recovered a strand of Maddy's hair from behind the sofa in the McCanns' apartment, which was being analysed by toxicologists at the Forensic Science Service laboratory in Birmingham, and which they said would prove that Maddy had been drugged. The McCanns were beginning to agree, as it explained why Maddy didn't scream out when she was taken, but were adamant that it would have been done by their kidnapper – not them. 'I really believe they [whoever took her] gave her a drug,' said Gerry's mother Eileen McCann. 'There is no way they carried her out of there without her waking. If she was taken when she was sleeping by somebody she did not know, she would have screamed the place down.'

The Portuguese police, needless to say, misinterpreted this. 'It is interesting that the McCanns are now saying they think their daughter was drugged,' said a source within the force. 'It is suspicious that they have found an explanation just as the evidence begins to build.'

In an astonishing development, the police were forced to remove Chief Inspector Goncalo Amaral off the case after an outburst against both the McCanns and the British police. Indeed, he was not only taken off the case, but was demoted to the rank of inspector and stripped of his role as regional head of the Policia Judiciaria. The British police, he'd said, were shielding the McCanns and only following up the leads that the McCanns wanted to be followed. He also said they were obstructing a proper investigation into the case.

The reason for this was an e-mail that had been sent to Prince Charles's website, alleging that Madeleine might have been snatched by a former employee of the Ocean Club at Praia da Luz. This had 'no credibility whatsoever,' said Amaral, before adding to the Portuguese paper *Diario de Noticias*, 'The British police have only been working on what the McCann couple want them to and what suits them most. The Ocean Club is in Praia da Luz, not in London. That means that anything in respect to the complex and the employees – current or ex – has been or is being investigated by the Policia Judiciaria. It won't be an email, and an anonymous one at that, which will distract our line of investigation.' He then claimed that the McCanns were behind the tip-off. It was, incidentally, forbidden under Portuguese law for him to talk about the case.

The clearly embarrassed Portuguese authorities acted fast. Amaral's boss, Alipio Ribeiro, removed him immediately. 'We cannot make any comment on the reasons for his dismissal,' said a Portuguese police spokesman. 'But we can confirm he did not resign. He was removed from his post. The decision was taken by the national leadership of the Judicial Police.' The Portuguese government was equally dismayed: Justice Minister Alberto Costa issued a public reprimand, the first time a member of the government had intervened in the case.

The McCanns remained silent. 'We are aware of what has happened and we simply cannot comment,' said their spokesman Clarence Mitchell. 'However, Kate and Gerry have constantly said they are very willing to co-operate fully with the Portuguese authorities. They will continue to do so regardless of who is in charge of the hunt for Madeleine.'

The sacking sparked some anger amongst Amaral's colleagues, who clearly saw the hands of the government in this. 'This was a political decision,' said one. 'Politicians should not interfere with a criminal investigation.' It emerged that he himself learned of his fate after receiving a fax that read simply, 'Transferred to Faro for convenience of the service' from Alipio Ribeiro, head of the Policia Judicaria. The transfer was announced just an hour and a half after the public reprimand from Alberto Costa, but it was hard to see how the force could have done anything else. Indeed, they might have been relieved to have the opportunity to put a new person in charge. A source close to the McCanns certainly saw it in that light: 'If whoever takes over the case were to say he'd like to meet them, they would do that, but it has not been discussed at the moment,' he said. 'They hope that the Portuguese authorities will see that the position is filled as urgently as possible because there is still a need for Madeleine to be found.'

Still, however, there was some resentment. 'He was a scapegoat for the English,' one unnamed colleague told the Portuguese newspaper *Correio da Manha*. Meanwhile, Carlos Anjos, president of the Judicial Police Inspectors' Union, blamed the British press for highlighting Amaral's long lunches. 'He was the victim of personal attacks by the British media, which not only questioned his honour as a policeman, but also attacked him as a human being,' he said.

The McCanns remained silent, but a friend spoke out. 'We would not presume to tell the Portuguese police how to do their job,' he said. 'The departure of one officer will not affect the volume of work at their disposal. But Kate and Gerry hope it will reinvigorate the search for Madeleine and move away from some of the recent distractions.'

Some hope. The Portuguese police's latest theory about Madeleine's disappearance was leaked to the press. They were still sure that she had been sedated by her parents, but had now decided that she woke up and went to find them. Befuddled by the drugs, she tripped and fell down a flight of ten steps leading from the patio to the street and died. However, this theory still had the McCanns concealing her body for over three weeks in the blazing Portuguese heat and then disposing of it in the Renault Scenic hire car, which was incredibly unlikely.

Amidst all the to-ing and fro-ing, it was sometimes hard to remember the actual human suffering the McCanns were going through. All of this was still not bringing back Madeleine, which is all they really wanted, and the depth of their pain was made clear in an interview with their local paper, the *Leicester Mercury*, on the five-month anniversary of the day Maddy disappeared. 'Sometimes the most trivial of things can bring you crashing down,' said Kate. 'I've had days when if I wasn't crying about Madeleine I was crying from the letters and messages of support people have sent us. They have kept us going on low days, kept us strong during the worst times. We can be out in the car and people will put their thumbs up. It's a simple thing, but we take great comfort from that. I don't think there has been one particular low moment. Obviously, nothing can compare with the night Madeleine went missing.

'A lot has happened since then. Time passed by so surreally. It was the first few hours, then eight hours, then twenty-four hours, forty-eight hours, then seventy-two hours … I don't remember. Each day felt like a week. The messages of support, friends and family rallying round – you just can't overestimate what those have meant for us.'

Gerry also spoke out. 'I went to the dump to throw some things away,' he said. 'Even there, people came up and said, "I hope everything works out all right for you". These were just ordinary, everyday people – people I did not know, people going about their business – taking time out to pass on their best wishes.'

As for when they were named as suspects, Gerry revealed that the pain they had felt when Madeleine was so great it helped them to deal with everything else. 'I think when we were made suspects in our own daughter's disappearance – when the inference was that Madeleine was dead and that, somehow, we were involved … But, no, it can't get worse than that first night. Everything that has happened, everything we do and feel, it is all put into perspective by how we felt on that first night. Despite everything that has been written, we're still receiving many messages of support. All the letters we have received have been positive. We've been getting three big crates of mail every day. It's so much we have to collect it from the post office. We didn't think it was fair on our post lady. We're still receiving a big box of letters every day. It's incredible.'

Gerry's colleagues were very supportive, holding a weekly vigil in which they prayed for Madeleine's safe return. 'They started during the first week of Madeleine's disappearance and they are still holding them now, every Friday lunchtime,' he said. 'That touches me. It keeps me going. I did think about going back to work in some capacity but that all changed when we were declared arguidos. That has put things back a bit. I won't be changing careers, let's say. The hospital has been incredibly supportive.'

So had many other sectors of the community, as Kate revealed. 'There are so many people to thank, the primary schools, the local police,' she said. 'They have been excellent, so pleasant. Our local church is a five-minute walk from our house. They have been saying prayers continually. In fact, people from all faiths have been praying. We have had support from the Anglican Church, from the Baptist Church.'

And people were still contributing to the 'Find Madeleine' fund: they had just received a cheque for £57,000. 'It's a huge amount,' said Gerry. 'Both Kate and I would like to say a big, sincere thank you to everyone who has been so supportive. It means a lot to us. We want to increase awareness, get back to basics if you like, target specific areas with pictures and billboards and messages. We want to refocus the coverage.' 'The coverage has been on us,' said Kate. 'The coverage should be on Madeleine, no one else.' 'The legal side has taken priority,' Gerry went on. 'We want to change that and refocus the attention on to finding Madeleine.'

In some ways, home life was returning to normality. The twins had settled back in again and, of course, remained unaware of the enormity of the search for their sister, although they did know something was going on. 'It didn't take them long to settle back,' said Kate. 'It's familiar for them at home, they have their toys, they know where things are. They're back in nursery; they play so well together. They miss their big sister. We tell them that she is missing and that everyone is looking for her. And that's the truth.'

'They don't dwell on it,' added Gerry. 'They miss her but they are not tormented by it. Time means nothing to them at their age. They have no comprehension of when things have happened. They're happy with themselves.'

'There is a semblance of normality returning,' said Kate. 'It's more normal than it was three weeks ago, Amelie and Sean see to that. But really how can it be normal? How can it be normal without Madeleine?'

A Police Farce

It had been hoped that with Goncalo Amaral off the case, there would be some progress in the hunt for Madeleine. In the event, the opposite proved to be the case. Tavares Almeida, Amaral's deputy, had been expected to take over the running of the investigation but, perhaps aware what a poisoned chalice it had become, two days after Amaral's departure, he applied for unpaid leave. It was given.

It was chaos and Alipio Ribeiro, Portugal's most senior policeman, knew it. 'There is a crisis every day, this one is resolved; let's see what tomorrow's is,' he said wearily. He didn't have long to wait. Despite global condemnation of the way the case had been run, the four remaining officers working on the case were ordered to take fifteen days' holiday by the end of the year.

'Since the case began, the team has been progressively reduced,' said a source to the 24 *Horus* daily newspaper, defending the move. 'Now there are half a dozen agents and they have not had holidays. The weariness of the agents can jeopardise the success of the investigation.'

Eyebrows were raised across the world, although this was in accordance with Portuguese law, which states that every worker must have a minimum of fifteen days holiday a year. But it also highlighted quite how small the team searching for Madeleine had become and the workload this reduced team of men had to bear.

'If the work that is normally done by six people is now done by five that means less productivity and a greater workload for those who stay,' said the source. 'Besides that, we also have to count the weekly days off to which each investigator has a right. This is too small a team for the demands of this case so it is very natural that from now on the investigations will slow down.'

The McCanns, as ever, were silent. 'We hope there always have been, are now and will continue to be, sufficient resources available in the search to find Madeleine,' said their spokesman Clarence Mitchell.

The reason for Tavares Almeida's rapid retreat from the scene soon became clear: like his former boss Goncalo Amarel, he was also to face charges relating to the way he treated a suspect. In this case, a rail worker from Sintra was arrested in connection with a wave of robberies in Lisbon, carried out by violent children from orphanages, who indulged in a mugging spree. Antonio Marinho, the rail worker in question, was ultimately cleared of any involvement in the gang, but alleged that he was badly beaten up in police custody, leaving him with four broken ribs and bruising to his throat, stomach and back.

Initially his allegations were played down, but he finally got the criminal court in Lisbon to demand that three of the eight detectives present were charged, including Almeida. And if that wasn't enough, the woman in charge of that investigation, Ana Paula Matos, was now on remand awaiting trial on charges of taking money recovered from drug dealers. It didn't exactly show the Portuguese police in a very flattering light.

Given the sensitivities of the case, when a new officer was chosen to lead the investigation, it was one of the most senior police officers in Portugal. He was Paulo Rebelo, the deputy director of the national force, and one of the first things he did was to order a new search of the apartment where the McCanns were staying. There was no doubt this search was thorough – it went on for a good five hours – but it was now over five months since Maddy had gone missing. It looked very much like a case of locking the stable door months after the horse had bolted.

But he was certainly a policeman with a good track record. He had served in drugs squads in Lisbon and Porto, and made his name at the Central Directory for the Investigation of Drug Trafficking, where he had become one of its four associate directors last year. He had also led the country's armed robbery unit and counter-terrorism team. More pertinently to the case of Madeleine, he had investigated claims of a child sex ring at a children's home, uncovering the notorious Casa Pia paedophile ring in 2002. He also headed the Mea Culpa investigation into the death of thirteen people in an arson attack.

The McCanns certainly hoped his involvement with the case would help them to make progress: 'Kate and Gerry hope Mr Rebelo will now work to eliminate them from the inquiry as suspects and will then be in a position to refocus his team into the search for Madeleine,' said Clarence Mitchell. 'We hope a new head of the inquiry will work to ensure the unsubstantiated and unfounded allegations surrounding the case will end.'

Rebelo certainly knew what was at stake. It was not just a small child that had to be found: he also had to rescue the reputation of the Portuguese police. This time there were to be no mistakes, no boozy lunches, no idiocies as there had been before. 'He will get tough - he knows the reputation of the Portuguese police force now hangs on this case,' said a source. 'He has said he will study every piece of evidence personally. In short, the investigation starts again today. There will be immediate action and it will involve some drama.'

But the ceaseless flow of rumour and innuendo did not come to a stop. The latest to do the rounds was that four more children had been present in the flat the night Madeleine disappeared, all children of the McCanns' friends. 'It's utter rubbish,' said Clarence Mitchell.

Meanwhile, there were developments, of a sort, in Britain. The British police had written to other tourists staying in the resort at the time, asking them to provide DNA samples. (Why the Portuguese police had not done this five months earlier, they were too polite to say.) Detective Superintendent Stuart Prior was the man in charge: he wrote to the tourists: 'I have now been asked by the Portuguese investigation team to arrange for DNA samples and fingerprints to be taken from holidaymakers living in the UK who were staying at the Ocean Club Resort.' The DNA and fingerprints 'will help the Portuguese police to eliminate samples they have taken and not yet been able to identify'.

And that was not all. The tourists were asked for details about whether they'd used their mobile phones; about their movements; and about the clothes they'd worn on the night in question. Unsurprisingly, some of them struggled to recall what the police wanted to know. 'They said that they would aim to do this kind of work within forty-eight hours of a disappearance and could not comprehend why it has taken five months,' said one of the tourists. 'We struggled to remember the kind of detail that they wanted about our movements on specific days and what we were wearing.'

But, as they had done so often in the past, matters now turned really nasty. It was already known that Madeleine's birth was the result of IVF treatment, and now suggestions were raised in the Portuguese press that Gerry was not Maddy's biological father. This, of course, would cause big problems with any DNA tests.

The McCanns were incensed. They were still not allowed to speak about the case, but they authorised an immediate statement from Clarence Mitchell. 'Due to further unwarranted, unsubstantiated and totally inaccurate speculation in the Portuguese press today, Gerry and Kate McCann and their lawyers have authorised me to issue the following statement,' he said. 'For the record, Gerry is the biological father of his daughter Madeleine. A newspaper report in the *24 Horus* newspaper suggesting otherwise is nothing short of lies. It is indeed an absolute fabrication. Gerry and Kate's lawyers in both Britain and Portugal would remind editors in both countries that they are monitoring coverage very closely and will not hesitate from taking action at the appropriate stage in either country when and wherever it's felt necessary.'

This really was pretty low stuff, and a measure of the desperation the Portuguese police now felt. Nor did it help in the search for Maddy. A state of virtual warfare now seemed to exist between the McCanns and the Portuguese police, something that was neither helpful to any of the parties concerned, nor necessary.

Further doubt was cast on the police's version of events when an international manhunt expert, Danie Krugel, who was known as 'The Locator', said he had managed to trace DNA evidence that led to the conclusion that Maddy had been taken out to sea. 'I spent four nights in July carrying out my searches', he said. 'I've been able to trace where Madeleine was in the resort and have drawn a map which has been given to the police. I can't reveal details, as I don't want to alert anyone who might try to disturb the scene. But I believe I've traced where she was taken that night and now it's down to police to use their search experts to do the rest. The area to which my investigation led me is a difficult one to search. We tried to contact the family at the very beginning to offer our help, but unfortunately we didn't get called in until a couple of months after Madeleine went missing.'

Indeed, Krugel had had some success in the past, and it was after hearing about him that the McCanns asked him for help. They gave him a strand of Maddy's hair, from which he traced a route from the holiday apartment down to the sea, a report that tallied with the McCanns' friend Jane Tanner's eyewitness account of seeing a man carrying a small child on the night that Maddy disappeared. It all pointed to Maddy being taken away by sea – but there the trail went cold.

The Portuguese police had been happy for the McCanns to call on the services of Danie Krugel, but unfortunately did not appear to have taken it any further. Krugel's findings pointed to clear evidence of abduction, but they, of course, had their own theories and were concentrating on those. There were also those who were happy to cast doubt on Mr Krugel's methods, which were kept a closely guarded secret: if he was really that good, they seemed to say, then why couldn't he find every person in the world that had gone missing? (It should be said he had a proven record involving a number of snatched children in South Africa.)

But even if he offered only a small chance for hope, the McCanns were clearly going to act on it. 'The work of Mr Krugel should not be underestimated and gives great hope to Gerry and Kate,' said a source close to the family. 'Many people have contacted the couple to try to help but while their hearts may be in the right place they just don't have the expertise to be of assistance. But Mr Krugel has a proven record of finding people and his methods are extremely credible.

'The results in Praia da Luz crucially match many other strands of the investigation which all point to Madeleine being abducted and still being alive on that night when she was taken. Kate and Gerry just want police to concentrate on this evidence and find Madeleine. It's so frustrating for them. It is important to mention Kate and Gerry used Mr Krugel with the full cooperation of Portuguese police. The fact they carried out searches as a result of his work prove his credibility with them. Yet sadly they [the Portuguese police] seem to have decided to no longer follow this line of inquiry.'

At least the arrival of Paulo Rebelo looked set to fire some fresh energy into the case. Clearly desperate to re-establish the reputation of the Portuguese police in the eyes of the world, he hit the ground running, doubling the numbers working on the investigation and bringing some of the country's top murder detectives to work on the case. The McCanns were clearly relieved.

'These are fresh eyes, for which they are grateful,' said Clarence Mitchell. 'The development is welcomed by the family. If the new team are experts in homicide then hopefully Mr Rebelo can eliminate Kate and Gerry as suspects.'

British police also welcomed the move. 'For a long time the investigation has lacked direction and impetus and he has brought that back,' said Mark Williams-Thomas, a former Surrey Police child protection officer, who has worked on some of the UK's largest murder and paedophile cases, including that of Sarah Payne. 'You wonder why they didn't bring him in earlier. It is absolutely right that they should revisit the location so they are familiar with it when they come to interviews. That shows that there is some proper detective work going on.'

One name that had been all but forgotten in this was Robert Murat's. But he was still an arguido, despite speculation over previous months that his name would be cleared and he, too, hoped that Rebelo's arrival would finally bring some closure to his own situation. As an official suspect, he was not allowed to speak directly about the case, but he could, at least, tell the BBC, 'It has been five months now, my savings are gone, and my mum has been doing what she can and it's just very, very difficult.'

His cousin, Sally Everleigh, was under no such constraints. 'It's five months down the line and he last heard from the police three months ago,' she said. 'It seems everything is against him. He has not seen his daughter at all. All his savings are gone, he needs to reclaim his life.'

Murat's friend Tuck Price also spoke up in his defence. 'He has not been cleared yet, but that's what the family are looking for now,' he said. 'There's a new person in charge and this now needs to happen. He should be the number one case because he was the first arguido. If they are going to be reviewing everything again, then his case needs to be heard because his life has been ruined by this.'

And now, five months after Maddy disappeared, the police, as well as the McCann family, were forced to confront the fact that they might never know what had happened. The McCanns had already said as much and now the police, as well as locals, working on the theory that Madeleine's body might have been dumped at sea, were saying the same thing. 'I personally looked in forty wells,' said local council chief Manuel Borba. 'I'm not going to say it's impossible the body has been hidden here – but I don't believe it has. If the body was thrown out to sea that night, it will never drift back to dry land.'

The leaks continued to the Portuguese press, again claiming the body was dumped at sea. 'The area around Luz was searched twice with a team of men and dogs,' said a police source. 'If her body had been thrown into a well, it would have been found. And earth that's been moved never goes unnoticed. Whoever had the expertise to make her disappear from the apartment also had the expertise to throw her into the sea.'

There were very few people who still really believed the McCanns had anything to do with the disappearance of their child, but some unpleasant sniping had been going on in the background, questioning how Kate seemed to know immediately that she'd been snatched, rather than simply wandered off. A very innocent explanation emerged: that she saw the imprint of her daughter's body on the sheets, and also saw Maddy's beloved Cuddle Cat, tucked up high, out of reach.

'People keep asking how did Kate know so quickly that Madeleine had been taken and not just walked out,' said a source close to the McCanns. 'But it's obvious. When she put Maddy to bed the child was all tucked up around the shoulders, and when Kate realised she was gone all the sheets were still neatly in place. A child of that age wouldn't have been able to get out of bed without moving a thing. Someone had clearly been in and carefully lifted her out. Kate realised that right away. This evidence must now refocus the police attention. Kate and Gerry should be released from their suspect status.'

The Portuguese police, desperate for something – anything – that would lead to a breakthrough in the case, turned to a South American psychic for help. Isabel Avila, from Chile, who was not asking for any money for her work, had drawn up a map to help the police. It placed Maddy near a bridge, with some tall antennas nearby. This was not actually as odd as it seemed: many police forces use people like Isabel, who have sometimes been known to help. Indeed, Isabel had helped other forces in the past: her maps had tracked at least seventy people, including a teenager who drowned in a flood, a six-year old child and forty-five soldiers who had died in a blizzard. 'This woman has a proven track record,' said Lucia Nuncio, a Portuguese diplomat currently serving in Chile.

The police agreed. 'This type of procedure is normal in complicated cases such as this one, which have been in the hands of the same people for a long time,' said a police source. 'People who are not familiar with the inner workings of an investigation have a different way of looking at things – and they can reach different conclusions.'

Isabel herself was unable to say whether Maddy was alive or dead, but said she would do what she could. 'She has always been in Portugal but in bad conditions,' she said. 'I have a very clear idea of what happened and I feel I can find her. I'm happy to travel to Portugal to the place where Madeleine disappeared to better detect her energy.'

To date, the case has had at least one happy outcome. It has focused the eyes of the Portuguese on the dreadful area of paedophilia, and in mid-October, the Portuguese police smashed the country's biggest ever paedophile ring. More than three hundred officers raided seventy-five homes and businesses at dawn, seizing computers and arresting eighty suspects, in a clampdown called 'Operation Predator'. It was not directly related to the McCann enquiry, but Paulo Rebelo ordered his team to liaise with the anti-paedophile squad to see if anything relating to Maddy came to light.

'We are naturally encouraged by news of such police activity and we would hope that any evidence that proves relevant to the search for Madeleine will be swiftly acted upon,' said Clarence Mitchell. A friend of the McCanns added: 'This shows the scale of the problem in Portugal, and appears to show that the Portuguese police seem to be looking in the right direction. It may provide vital leads.'

Will the case ever be solved? It is impossible to say. Children go missing every year and, to the great anguish of all involved, their fate is not always known. Sometimes there are cases, like Maddy's, that catch the public eye because they are so very strange and because the child is so very appealing: Ben Needham, who vanished aged twenty-one months on the Greek island of Cos in 1991, is one such. His mother Kerry, now thirty-five, who lives with her twelve-year-old daughter Leighanna in Sheffield, had some very unhappy memories awakened by Maddy's case.

'When Ben vanished there was just me, my mum and dad and we did the best we could to keep the case going but we got very little help,' she said. 'I was 19, a naïve girl from a council estate. People thought, "she will go away in a few months, have another child and forget about it". I did have another child but I've not forgotten and I won't go away. Not a day goes by when I don't think of him.'

She had also seen Kate McCann on television: 'It was

like a mirror image, the haunting look, the fear,' she said. 'It was like seeing myself sixteen years ago. I'll never give up looking for Ben. All I want is to see him again so he knows the truth. Ben, I'll always be here for you.'

At least the police didn't try to say that she was involved. Another person the case also awoke memories for was Lindy Chamberlain-Creighton, the Australian mother who was jailed for life after her two-month-old baby, Azaria, vanished during a camping trip to the outback. The parents believed that a dingo snatched Azaria. No body was ever found, and Lindy was eventually released in 1988 after some of Azaria's clothing came to light.

'What that couple are going through sounds like a mirror image to what happened to me,' said Lindy, now 59. 'Lie and tell us you did it, and you can go free, tell us the truth and you can't, the police will be saying.'

What really happened to Maddy? The great probability is that she was snatched on the night she vanished and taken out to sea. Everything points to it: the man seen carrying a child, the DNA trail that led down to the beach. After that, it is impossible to say. Although the wrong child was spotted on several occasions, there are still credible reports that she might be in Spain or Morocco.

It is a sad story that has caused terrible anguish to Maddy's parents, showed the Portuguese police in a dreadful light and destroyed the reputation of someone who in all likelihood is an innocent man. Very few people have emerged with credit, although Kate and Gerry McCann are two of them: under almost intolerable strain, first from losing their daughter, and then from being named as suspects themselves, they have behaved with consistent dignity.

If anything comes out of this, it is, perhaps, the plight of the children that go missing every year. The vast majority of these cases never reach a wider public and Maddy's case has, at least, brought the problem to the fore. In the longer term, the Find Madeleine fund may well be used to look for other children who have gone missing and there has been talk that Kate herself might one day work in that field.

But above all, Maddy's story remains a mystery. For all the public censure about leaving the children alone, pictures of the resort at Praia da Luz show that the parents could see the apartment where their children were sleeping that night, and that what happened to Maddy was, above all else, simply terribly bad luck. As for all the stories about the McCanns hiding her and disposing of her over three weeks later, it simply doesn't ring true. They were in the scorching heat, under the eyes of the world. It would be strange indeed if they did what they were alleged to have done.

The Portuguese police, of course, have some soul searching to do, as well. They might dwell upon the fact that not only has their incompetence been made clear to the world, but that their cruelty has, too. They might not have beaten Kate and Gerry to extract a confession, as some of them are alleged to have done in other cases, but the fact remains that they took two suffering parents and pulled their reputations through the mire. The allegation that Gerry was not Maddy's biological father was the lowest point in this, and it is thought that once they have been cleared of arguido status, the couple intends to sue.

But in the middle of all this controversy, it's easy to lose sight of the main fact of the case, namely that a little girl went missing from a popular holiday resort not far from where her parents were dining, and that no one, no one at all, really has any idea what happened to her. The police may roar; the rest of the world looks on in dismay. For the simple truth is this: Madeleine McCann has not yet been found.